Shadow Lands

Johannes Bobrowski

Shadow Lands

Selected Poems

Translated by Ruth & Matthew Mead
with an Introduction by Michael Hamburger

A NEW DIRECTIONS BOOK

The Publishers thank Deutsche Verlags-Anstalt, Stuttgart, and Union Verlag
(VOB), Berlin, for permission to use poems translated in their editions of
Johannes Bobrowski's poems: for poems in part one, from *Sarmatische Zeit,*
© 1961 by Deutsche Verlags-Anstalt, except "Prussian Elegy," ©1961 by
Union Verlag; for poems in part two, from *Schattenland Ströme,* © 1962 by
Deutsche Verlags-Anstalt; for poems in part three, from *Wetterzeichen,*
© 1966 by Union Verlag. Some of these translations appeared in *Shadow
Land* (Donald Carroll, 1966), the Penguin Modern European Poets *Selected
Poems* of Johannes Bobrowski and Horst Bienek (1971), and *From the Rivers*
(Anvil, 1975). The poem "Translator to Translated" first appeared in
Matthew Mead's *Identities and other poems* (Rapp & Carroll, 1967).

Manufactured in the United States of America.
New Directions Books are printed on acid-free paper.
First published in Great Britain in 1984 by Anvil Press Poetry Ltd.
First published as a New Directions Paperbook Original 788 in 1994.
Published simultaneously in Canada by Penguin Books Canada Limited.

Library of Congress Cataloging-in-Publication Data
Bobrowski, Johannes, 1917-1965.
        Shadow lands: selected poems / Johannes Bobrowski ; translated
by Ruth & Matthew Mead ; introduction by Michael Hamburger.
            p. cm.
        Includes index
        ISBN 0-8112-1276-9 (alk. paper)
        I. Mead, Ruth.   II. Mead, Matthew, 1924-   III. Title.
PT2603.013S45   1994
831'.914-dc20
                                                            94-9979
                                                            CIP

New Directions Books are published for James Laughlin
by New Directions Publishing Corporation
80 Eighth Avenue, New York 10011

Contents

INTRODUCTION by Michael Hamburger   11
Translator to Translated   19

from **Sarmatian Time** (1961)

Call   23

I
Village   24
Childhood   25
Nymph   26
The Jura   27
The Wives of the Nehrung-Fishers   29
Fishingport   30
To the Jewish Dealer A.S.   31
The Road of the Armies   32
Wagon Trip   34
The Log-Cabin Above the Vilia   35
Vilna   36
By the River   38
The Lithuanian Well   39
Graveyard   40
Dead Language   41
The Spoor in the Sand   42
Lithuanian Songs   43
The Sarmatian Plain   44
Counterlight   46

II
Pruzzian Elegy   47

III
Mourning for Jahnn   49
Villon   50
Góngora   51
Günderode   52
Joseph Conrad   53
Dylan Thomas   54

IV
The Singing Swan   55

Windmill   56
Village Road   57
The Church: Comfort My Affliction   58
On the Tauric Road   59
Landscape with Birds   60
Steppe   61
Lake Ilmen 1941   62
River Poem   63
The Homeland of the Painter Chagall   65
Latvian Songs   66
The Duna   67
Nightway   68
Kaunas 1941   69
The Hawk   71
Return   72
Fire and Snow   73
Lake Shore   74
One Day   75
The Memel   76
The Daubas   78
Winterlight   80

Recall   82

from **Shadowland Rivers** (1962)

The Call of the Quail   85

    I
The Eagle   87
Plain   88
Calls   89
Dryad   90
At the River   91
Summer Cries   92
Unsaid   93
Tale   94
The Wanderer   95
The Animals at Christmas   96
Winter Cries   97
The Death of the Wolf   98
Hamann   99
Elder–Blossom   100
To the Chassid Barkan   101

Memorial Leaf   102
Weathersigns   103

II
Lament   105
Sea-Piece   106
French Village   107
Brentano in Aschaffenburg   108
Hölderlin in Tübingen   109
Night-Swallows   110
From the Rivers   111
Bird Routes 1957   113
Gertrud Kolmar   114
Else Lasker-Schüler   115
To Nelly Sachs   116

III
The Don   118
Ikons   119
Deserted Township   120
Under the Edge of Night   121
North Russian Town   122
In Transit   123
Above the River   124
Cathedral 1941   125
Village Church 1942   126
Report   127
Cloister Near Novgorod   128
The Tomsk Road   129
Easter   130
Russian Songs   131
In Memory of B.L.   132
The Ford   133
Log-Cabin   134
Village Music   135
The Road Home   136
Always to be Named   137

Mickiewicz   138

from **Weathersigns** (1966)

J. S. Bach   143
Pike Time   144
Mozart   145

Midstream   146
Midnight Village   147
The Latvian Autumn   148
With Wings   149
Novgorod (Arrival of the Saints)   150
Shadow Land   152
To Klopstock   153
Experience   154
Encounter   155
Tolmingkehmen Village   156
Towpath   157
Meadowbrook   158
Sanctuary   159
The Volga Towns   160
With Your Voice   161
The End of the Summer Night   162
Calamus   163
The Towns on the Baltic Sea   164
The Water   165
Exodus of the Gods   166
Language   167
In the Empty Mirror   168
When the Rooms   169
Place of Fire   170
Birdsnest   171
Jakub Bart in Ralbitz   172
Arrival   173
Answer   175
Nightfisher   176
Beachcomber   177
Names for the Persecuted   178
To Jawlensky   179
By Day   180
Esther   181
Crypt/Brandenburg Cathedral   182
Town   183
Kolno Dance   184
The Bird, White   185
House   186
Reawakening   188
Silcher's Grave   189
With the Songs of Sappho   190
The Deserted House   191

Precaution   192
Undine   193
Blood Rain   194
Mobile by Calder   195
Estrangement   195
To Hölty   196
The Word "Man"   197

NOTES   199

JOHANNES BOBROWSKI: A NOTE   203

INDEX OF TITLES   205

Introduction

ON MARCH 18th 1963 Johannes Bobrowski wrote to me: "A Mr Matthew Mead . . . informs me that he has translated the greater part of my published poems, and asks whether I already have plans for an English translation." That was the beginning of my association with the excellent versions of excellent poems now collected in this book. When both Christopher Middleton and I had assured Bobrowski that Matthew Mead was a good poet, those early translations, drawn from Bobrowski's two published collections, were submitted to the two of us for checking and judgement, which proved unreservedly positive. The only exception, I think, was poems in classical metres, still omitted from Ruth and Matthew Mead's selection. "German Alcaics and Asclepiads in English – that, it seems to me, amounts to magic – if quite naturally flowing verses are to result. (With mine, in the second collection, something seemed not quite right to me in Mead's versions.)" That was Bobrowski's comment a few months later, after I had sent him my Hölderlin versions, including many Alcaics and Asclepiads. (Bobrowski's "Ode on Thomas Chatterton", one of the poems in question, is in the Sapphic metre.) The outcome, in any case, was that both Middleton and I recommended Ruth and Matthew Mead's versions for authorization, though both of us might be sorely tempted to poach – as I was to do only once, for special and unavoidable reasons, and only over poems that the Meads had not translated.

Publication was a different matter. "Christopher Middleton wrote to me that the prospects of finding a publisher for them are dubious. That is just what I should have supposed", Bobrowski reported to me on April 16th. Even in West Germany Bobrowski had become known as a poet only in 1960, when a number of his poems appeared in the anthology *Deutsche Lyrik auf der anderen Seite* (German Poetry on the Other Side); but the destinies of Bobrowski's books proved as unpredictable and incomparable as the work itself. By 1966 Ruth and Matthew Mead's translations had not so much found as been found by a publisher, Donald Carroll, who – against all the odds even in a decade that now looks like a golden age for poetry in Britain – set up a new firm mainly in order to publish *Shadow Land*. Within a year this book by an almost unknown German poet, from a small press totally unknown, was sold out and had to be reprinted. That, too, amounted to magic, contrary as it was to all Middleton's and my experiences with translations from the German.

My friendship and correspondence with Johannes Bobrowski had begun only in December 1962, when I crossed over from West Berlin to attend a reading by him under the auspices of the Lutheran Academy of Berlin-Brandenburg, after being won over by what I had been able to obtain of his early publications. Between the appearance of his first book of poems in 1960 and that first meeting, Bobrowski had established himself in both Germanies as a greatly admired poet. Between 1962 and his early death in 1965, Bobrowski wrote the two novels and three collections of short prose texts that were to add to his reputation, as well as continuing to write the poems posthumously collected in his third book of poems. (His fourth collection, *Im Windgesträuch*, published in 1970 and not represented here, consists of poems written in the fifties and of later poems never finished to Bobrowski's satisfaction. Another posthumous book, *Literarisches Klima* (1977), collecting the satirical distichs that had served him as an alternative to the literary criticism or polemics he did not write, was also a product of those prolific years.)

To re-read the letters Bobrowski wrote to me during our all too brief friendship was to be struck above all by his presentiments of an early death. His constant awareness of it bears not only on the urgency that made him so productive as a prose writer at this period – though he remained a part-time writer, keeping regular office hours at the publishing house that employed him as a reader – but also on the very nature of his poems. In two letters Bobrowski told me that he wrote every poem as though it were to be his last. Quite apart from explicit references to his own death in the poems, or celebrations of it, as in "Village Music", the awareness is so pervasive throughout the poetry as to offer one clue to its peculiar impersonality, sustained even where a seemingly biographical first person singular operates in a poem; and this impersonality, or trans-personality, sets his poetry apart from most of that written in his time. It is part of that dimension of larger space, larger time, in which all Bobrowski's persons, places and things have their being, regardless of whether he drew them from observation or imagination, from history or from pre-historic myths.

Not all of Bobrowski's poems celebrate the Eastern European regions and figures with which his work as a whole will always be associated. His sympathies and affinities extended to France and Spain, and to Dylan Thomas's South Wales, just as they ranged from the Babylon and Assyria of the ancient epic *Gilgamesh* – a concern he shared with Peter Huchel – through the Middle Ages to his own century; but, with very few exceptions, all the writers, painters and composers to whom he devoted poems were dead. In that sense his poetry is consistently elegiac, almost as though death, for Bobrowski, had been a precondition for celebration; but, because continuities beyond death are what holds his work together, it is celebration, not mourning, that his poems just as consistently convey.

"My dark is already come" is the last line of the poem "Kaunas 1941", an early poem from Bobrowski's first book, about the German soldiers serving in Russia and the Jews exterminated by the régime they served. The guilt of the first person singular of that poem is conveyed in the question: "Did my eyes avoid yours/brother?" Whether we identify that person with the poet, who was such a soldier at the time, makes no difference to the poem, because Bobrowski did not write "confessional" poems, to get the guilt off his own chest. Yet the impact of the last line would not have the power it has if Bobrowski had transferred the personal guilt to a collective "we", since guilt – or anything else, for that matter – cannot be enacted or felt, only professed, collectively; and it was indeed for Bobrowski that his "dark was already come", so that every poem he wrote had to be written as though it were to be his last. The "I" in Bobrowski's poems – and any number of other instances could have been picked out – is a

13

functional and representative person, not an autobiographical one; but it had to be singular at the same time, rendering his own truth, his own experience, in the hope that others might recognize it as theirs.

It may be that Bobrowski knew his health to have been irreparably damaged during his years of military service in Russia or his protracted detention there as a prisoner-of-war, which did not end until 1949; but, if so, his robust appearance and habits belied the knowledge. His friends knew him as a man who enjoyed his food and drink, preferred a strong demotic brand of cigarettes that had to be brought to him from West Germany, always found time not only for his four children and work in the garden, but also for the many visitors who called on him in later years. Though he mentioned passing ailments in his letters, his death came to them as a sudden and unexpected blow; and its cause was an illness normally curable with an antibiotic.

Everything about Johannes Bobrowski was anomalous and unpredictable on one plane, all of a piece and straightforward on another. This Christian poet living in a Marxist State owed his relative exemption from ideological and bureaucratic pressures to an anomaly in the constitution, the continued existence of an opposition party, the Christian-Democratic Union, whose officially licensed publishing house both employed him and published his works. He chose to live in a suburb, Friedrichshagen, which in Imperial days had been a kind of Berlin Chelsea or Hampstead, favoured by artists and intellectuals, and seemed almost untouched and unchanged by the three drastic revolutions of the intervening half-century. To arrive there on the S-Bahn from West Berlin was like a journey in the time machine. Not even parked cars or traffic noises, let alone neon lights and hoardings, impinged on the anachronistic tranquillity of its houses and gardens. Bobrowski's household, too, maintained an old-fashioned order and decorum. Beside the many new books and works of art, especially graphics, piled up in the living room there was a small library of older books that were his true centre and base, including the Greek ones from which he translated only for his own pleasure; and the clavichord on which he played the music he liked best, mainly Buxtehude and Bach. Outwardly – and outside his home – Bobrowski was as plain and uncomplicated as he could make himself – the "bloke" of Ruth and Matthew Mead's version of "Village Music", a poem that stands out as being in the folk mode – a man quietly efficient in the office, convivial and even boisterous at literary or social gatherings. His spirituality, like his acute sensitivity and his erudition, was something he kept to himself.

Bobrowski's poems, too, were bound to seem wholly anomalous and unexpected to their first readers in both Germanies. East German poetry was expected to be either rhetorically and hortatorily "forward-looking", in the manner of Johannes R. Becher, or wrily and drily matter-of-fact and no-nonsense, in the manner of the later Brecht. (The exceptions were mostly poets of an older generation, like Erich Arendt, whose work was introduced to West German readers in the same anthology, or Peter Huchel, the only East German poet to whom Bobrowski's art was indebted and related. Personal relations between Huchel and Bobrowski were troubled by the circumstance that Huchel, who had published poems by Bobrowski in his magazine *Sinn und Form*, was disgraced and silenced after 1962, just when Bobrowski was being honoured and acclaimed in both Germanies. In a letter to me of March 1964, Bobrowski mentioned that he had "celebrated a reunion with Huchel – and it was high time, too"; but Huchel remained bitter in later years about Bobrowski's failure to stand up for him in public.) That any poet of his generation on either side of the Wall could claim the eighteenth-century poet Klopstock as his "teacher", as Bobrowski did, seemed more anomalous in West Germany than in East Germany, when to be "modern" and "avant-garde" was all the rage there. Klopstock – regarded as the "German Milton" at one time – had been a model for Hölderlin in his youth, but had been overshadowed by Goethe and Schiller in his lifetime, by the later Hölderlin ever since the rediscovery of that poet's work. Bobrowski's other eighteenth-century allegiance, to the prose writer Hamann, on whom he planned to write a book, was more understandable on regional grounds, because Hamann, "the

Magus of the North", was bound up with that "Sarmatian" world which Bobrowski had made his peculiar domain.

In fact, Bobrowski's affinity with Klopstock would scarcely have occurred to any reader of his poems if he had not pointed it out. His few classicizing odes are closer formally to Hölderlin's than to Klopstock's; and his free verse is even farther removed from Klopstock in its rhythms, structure, imagery and tone. The crux of the matter is that the Christian faith to which Bobrowski's professed allegiances to both Klopstock and Hamann do point might also have been less than obvious to many of his readers if he had not drawn attention to it in one of his few, and widely circulated, comments on his own work, because it was Bobrowski's distinction to leave his commitments implicit in his poems. More often than not, his commitments lie between the lines of his verse, in the choice and juxtaposition of his plain words and the peculiar syntax in which they are suspended. Any attentive reader will sense that there is more going on in Bobrowski's poems than meets the eye or the ear; but few even of those readers at home in the tradition – an imperilled one – that Bobrowski's work renewed might have known what it was, if Bobrowski had not issued his statement:

I began to write near Lake Ilmen in 1941, about the Russian landscape, but as a foreigner, a German. This became a theme, something like this: the Germans and the European East – because I grew up around the river Memel, where Poles, Lithuanians, Russians and Germans lived together, and among them all, the Jews – a long story of misfortune and guilt, for which my people is to blame, ever since the days of the Order of Teutonic Knights. Not to be undone, perhaps, or redeemed, but worthy of hope and honest endeavour in German poems. I have been helped in this by the example of a master, Klopstock.

Even if the statement, too, did not make Bobrowski's commitment quite as explicit as it became in some of his narrative prose, such as the novel *Levins Mühle*, it does tell us something both about the urgency I have mentioned and about the anomaly of poems written as an act of expiation. There may be still more secret links between the two. If so, they were "heart-mysteries", into which I have no wish to pry.

Thematically, Bobrowski's poems could not be forward-looking, since they evoke a world changed beyond recognition by political, social and economic upheavals and the extermination of whole peoples and cultures – from the ancient Pruzzians, whose pre-Christian gods and heroes are named in the poems, to the Jews and Gipsies. This Sarmatian world of Bobrowski's – a world imaginatively reassembled from fragments, memories, relics and unchanged landscapes in the poems – is as unfamiliar to most German readers not born in the extreme Eastern confines of the Second or Third Reich as it is to most English-speaking readers. (As Matthew Mead pointed out in his Introduction to the Penguin Bobrowski/Bienek selection, "the territory of the German Democratic Republic", which we call East Germany, "is properly *Mitteldeutschland*", Central Germany, since those Eastern regions were lopped off after the Second World War.) Nor should the "hope" in Bobrowski's statement be identified with that "principle of hope" which the dissident Marxist philosopher Ernst Bloch, at one time a fellow citizen of Bobrowski's, tried to uphold in the teeth of political realities. Bobrowski's hope was that he might succeed poetically in bearing witness to that vanished world; perhaps creating a kind of utopia also in the process, a model state projected into the past, rather than the future, but exemplary all the same, because utopias are not history, and the past has the advantage of providing more palpable material for poems. "Die Liebe" (Love) "is a tributary of the Vistula", Bobrowski wrote into the copy he gave me of *Levins Mühle*, connecting his topography of the vanished world with his implicit commitment, expiation, witness and redemption, by a factual entry on a river's name in a standard encyclopedia, Brockhaus. The ambiguity is a key to his poetry also, to its sober precision of detail on one level, its almost limitless expansiveness of meaning and suggestion on the other.

Ruth and Matthew Mead's versions have already proved that this combination of qualities can get across to readers in another language without more critical apparatus than Bobrowski and his translators have provided in brief factual notes. Knowing that the essence of these poems can be communicated even when this or that allusion remains obscure, to persons with no more first-hand knowledge of Bobrowski's Sarmatian background than I have, I conclude with the hope that this larger collection of Bobrowski's poems in English will meet with the attention it deserves in the very different "literary climate" of the 1980s. Unpredictable as it has always been, and impervious as it remains to changes of climate, literary and otherwise, Bobrowski's magic may well work once more.

MICHAEL HAMBURGER
Suffolk, August 1983

Translator to Translated

IN MEMORIAM JOHANNES BOBROWSKI

River, plain,
tree, the bird
in flight, habitation
and name, strange
to me, never strange
to you – the child's
eye, the soldier's
step, the known
threshold.

I crossed the plain
slowly, saw your fire
in the distance.
Have I set the tree
askew on your sky,
does your bird hover
strangely?
Love
translates
as love.
Her song sung
in a strange land.

An air that kills.

MATTHEW MEAD

from *Sarmatian Time*

Call

Vilna, you
oak –
my birch,
Novgorod –
once in the woods the cry
of my springs flew up, my days'
step sounded over the river.

O, it is the bright
glitter, the summer constellation,
given away; by the fire
squats the teller of tales,
those who listened nightlong, the young ones,
went away.

Lonely he will sing:
Across the steppe
wolves travel, the hunter
found a yellow stone,
it flared in the moonlight. –

What is holy swims,
a fish,
through the old valleys, the wooded
valleys still, the fathers'
words still sound:
Welcome the strangers!
You will be a stranger. Soon.

Village

Still the strange land
like drums, distant.
I come down the road.
Under the field-birch
the shepherd, in the rustle of leaves, in the rain-sound
of a cloud. Towards evening
a song of measured tones,
low cries
by the bushes.

Village between marsh and river,
bleak in your early winter's
crow-light – the road around the alders
overgrown, the huts soft with the stain
of rain and peat-smoke – you
my unending light,
my lacklustre light,
written on the edges
of my life, you old light.

Image of the hunter, conjuration,
animal-headed,
painted in the icy
cave, in the rock.

Childhood

Then I loved
the oriole –
the toll of bells sounded
above, sank low
through the greenwood,

when we squatted at the edge of the wood,
threaded red berries
on a grass-blade; the grey Jew
went by
with his cart.

At noon then the beasts stood
in the alders' black shadows
flicking away the flies
with angry tails.

Then the streaming rain-flood
fell from the open
sky; after all that darkness
the drops tasted
like earth.

Or the lads came
along the towpath with the horses,
on the shining brown
backs they rode laughing
across the deep.

Behind the fence
hummed clouds of bees.
Later the silver rattle of fear
ran through the thorn thicket
by the reedy lake.
It grew wild, a hedge,
darkening window and door.

Then the old woman sang in her
fragrant chamber. The lamp
hummed. The men
entered calling over their shoulders
to the dogs.

Night, long interlocked with silence –
time, slipping away, bitterer,
lasting from verse to verse:
childhood –
then I loved the oriole.

Nymph

Time of the cicadae, white
time, when the boy sat by
the water, resting
a round forehead on his arms. Where
has he gone?

There are ways
through the wood,
hidden. I fetch a bleeding
herb, lay it upon the stones,
mimic the light racing cry
of the jay at the field's edge.

And with a glance of green
she rises in the soft
spray of aldershadow.
Syrinx, your "O", a clatter
breaks through the bushes.

The Jura

Your waters
hard by the wood,
drifting depths,
full of the white cold of springs
in summer.
Only at noon
the fish with glancing fins
rises softly
to the surface,
an old robber. He returns
under the moon. And he does not hasten
when the wild otter
in the network of roots
plunges deep in the tangle of darkness.

In the great stillness
I come to you,
beautiful brother of woods and hills,
my river.
In the stillness of young day
I come down the sand-track
through the berried bushes. My boat
follows your heartbeat, the always
abrupt sound of water
under the coolness.

Willows, bitter smell,
a green as from the mists.
And the dew. There in the bushes
on the overgrown slope in front of the village
he squats grey-headed, with clammy
fingers he paints your red, your green, the strange
blue, the silver sound.

Once
a hard–mouthed god
of the fields lifted
his face. Standing above
the riverwood,
glistening with fat
in the black place of sacrifice,
he saw in the meadow the reddish ore;
and the springs broke forth,
the sandy track
of his glance.

Who lights the late
fires of the year, where the river
Nemona flows, cries out with straining lungs
before the falling ice? Out of open skies
it falls, a yellow smoke
travels before it.

The Wives of the Nehrung-Fishers

Where the Haff
lay dark round the beach,
while it was still night,
they rose from rustling
straw. They saw the boats
on the sea, distant.

When the boats came – the old men
watched at the rudder, the sons
dazed with sleep, the drag
of the nets in their arms –
a bright strip of dawn
moved through the sky
and hung round the roofs.
Above
a few calls
drifted in the wind.

And the catch was poor.
Once, they say,
herring in countless shoals
glittered around the bay; silvery
they vanished. The hag
shouts it mindlessly
at the edge of the wood –
old song, storm
wrenches it from the blue.

Fishingport

At evening
before the boats go
out, one after the other,
then I love you.

Until the morning
I love you with straw in the chamber,
with the land–wind over the roof,
with the hedge before your house,
with the dogs barking
before it is light.

My face tainted with fish, in dew
I shall come, one
whose hot hands
squander warmth on the silver form of
night. Here he comes
with his salty mouth. Now
he jumps into the last boat.

To the Jewish Dealer A.S.

I am from Rasainen.
That is where you spend the second night
in the wood when you come from the river,
where the woods open
and yellowish sand
presses up in the meadows.

There the nights are light.
Our wives extinguish the fires
early. We breathe
long and deep with the dark
aimless sigh of the wind.

All we have,
we have from the hands of the fathers.
Their care keeps us awake.
Their starry fear
shines in the tree of our speech.
Freezing we close graves
for them. The clouds loiter
long above, smoke.

Someone is always leaving,
does not look back, no waving
follows him. Yet the old men's
sayings at the gateposts still hold him
over the ocean. The sad music
of roads lined with birches
wakes him in the distant land.

The Road of the Armies

Aloof on the broken road,
in the crows' tracks on the snow,
drove the Corsican, a southern emperor,
shrunken with anger, –
overtaken at evening
by holy curses. The hungry
wolves dragged nights
of marsh-haze after him.

Yet the blue autumn
reaches for village and cloud.
Now, paths of home,
your beauty is like tears.
Sandy paths, the years
have stepped you out.

Years, tree-breaking winters,
when we listened for the light,
singing over the fire;
leant hard on the rock
of darkness and looked
for the dancing islands of the southern seas.

And we thirst.
Thus your heart, home,
has become a well
for us, smelled
in the sap of birches,
in the ferny golden nest
of your snakes.
Thus have your sons
with shadowy eyes
always returned to love
from foreign tables. –

Once,
here on the dark slope,
Orpheus walked. The wood
resounds eternally
with his lament.

Ah, the earth fooled
the singer; the many-voiced
Eurydice, from ravine,
from waters. She bows
our backs deeper in the
dank weed, before the year
goes out, with showers,
with angry rain.

Wagon Trip

Lovely moon of Mariampol! On your
strawy edge, my little town,
behind your market stalls
she rises,
heavy, and sags a little. The way
the horse-dealer walks, he buys
his mother a tasselled shawl.

At evening
late
they both sang. We drove
home across the river,
at the ferry with call
and answering call
the talk ran like water,
easy – and we listened long to her
over the town,
above in the towers, listened
to the Jewish moon. She is
like rue, the little
herb of tears and kisses
in the garden corner, our girls
pluck it.

————

Yoneleit, come, do not
lose your shawl. The old are sleeping.
Another night
sung to an end.

The Log-Cabin Above the Vilia

Riverwood,
dark with the cry of owls, in the crickets'
moss–white song, we
once saw the house on the shore,
grey in the beetle–fire
of mallows. Before the winter
came, a foreign snow swirled round us.

Log-cabin, the woods'
life and lovely transience,
lifted with wings
through the wind
as if over seas
you are come,
now the children
dwell in your smoke,
hear your sounds.

Your silence, the smell of leek
and the nettles' bitter
sharpness, the coolness of the well –
friend, once we lived
above the river, on the forest's
shadowed edge. With linked
hands let us sing,
sing again of the old house.

Throw a wreath over your
shoulder like the girls.
Call down the road; there ought to be an evening wind
rising in the birches, there ought to be
a fog moving easily up from the shore, the damp
circling the house –
when we sing with linked hands
of the old time,
loudly of girls,

softly of the wood
of the animals outside,
of the horses on grassy slopes.

It was dark, we walked
beneath the birches. At nights
the smugglers passed
with muffled steps. At new moon
once
the stranger stood in the yard.
"How do you live?" he asked. Alinka
sat in the window.
"With unbolted doors!" she cried.

Vilna

Vilna, you ripe elder!
With green eyes
your wolf-time is lost.
Aurochs and bear and boar
– when the cry of Giedimin's horn
surprised them, they halted only
at the Njemen, panting, gazing down
from the oak-wood above the banks.
Mickiewicz has sung the wild
light of the days;
and the dusk. But the gentle
Vilia glided easily.

Oh, the sky! a white
fluttering cloth swung beautifully
by the village songs.
The birch-dances bright
away into the fields.

But Lizdejko sings
no more, the bearded one sleeps,
they say, in the endlessly washed
sand of the shore – where out of the lake
Trakai rose, the dark
castle from the shimmer of Foretime.

His songs, like the heavy
banks, wooded, old,
which wander toward the Vilia,
like her skipping
gait, and the winds of Vilna, smoky,
coiled round the head
of the glorious daughter.

City of kings, all
the plains sing forever,
all the white plains, bitter
with the blood of sons,
sing to you with the whitebeard's
resounding voice, like the breaking
up and drifting of the ice,
with the sad songs of your Jews
at their feasts,
with the red sough of the pines.

By the River

You came
the moon-way, you came down
from Ostra Brama, from the glow
of the old icon, your arms
wrapped in your apron. You came
down the road to the river.

Light of evening, transient
toil out of dust,
always under the windfall
and gone in the swallow's glide.

Girl,
your look from the reeds.
I called you all day long.
Fill my hands with sand,
I want the moistness, the heaviness.
Now we breathe deeper the darkness.

Did I hear the bird over
the river? or the groundfish
below? – "Dearest, I always
hear the plop of fishes
and, above, the wing-beat.
Do not go from me."

The Lithuanian Well

My roads of sand, the sky
above the willow bushes.
Well–pole, rise!
Quench me with earth.

Hour-wide, lark, your song,
above the hawk.
When the sower hears you
the reaper has forgotten.

Look into the fallen field,
the wagons coming, the cry of the wind.
Goddess, lean back in the light.
Sing till your lips are pale.

Graveyard

Spears and stakes
against the sky, banners of moss,
a little wood
runs down the hill.
An army. Old.
The mouths full of grass.

Mouths which once sang.
Now broken bugles
sound amid snarl and rattle. Go now
to hear one voice
through the oar-beat over the water,
a simple call,

which, from the copse,
winter, the hidden one,
hurls back.

Dead Language

He with the beating wings
outside who brushes the door,
that is your brother, you hear him.
Laurio he says, water,
a bow, colourless, deep.

He came down with the river,
drifting around mussel
and snail, spread like a fan
on the sand and was green.

Warne he says and *wittan*,
the crow has no tree,
I have the power to kiss you,
I dwell in your ear.

Tell him you do not
want to listen –
he comes, an otter, he comes
swarming like hornets, he cries,
a cricket, he grows with the marsh
under your house, he whispers
in the well, *smordis* you hear,
your black alder will wither,
and die at the fence tomorrow.

The Spoor in the Sand

The pale old man
in the faded kaftan.
The prayer-curl as always.
I knew your house then, Aaron.
You carry the ashes
away in your shoe.

My brother drove
you from the door. I went
after you. How the skirt
swished round your feet. I found
a spoor in the sand.

Then I saw you
sometimes in the evening
coming from the firebreak,
whispering.
With your white hands
you scattered snow like seed
over the roof of the barn.

Because your fathers' god
will brighten the years
for us, Aaron,
the spoor lies
in the dust of the street,
and I find you.
And go.
And I bear your distance,
your expectation,
on my shoulder.

Lithuanian Songs

In the night, animal-eyed, I am
a bush, a tree by day,
a water in midday shadow,
grass in the sunlight.

Or as evening falls
a church on a hill, where my beloved,
a white priest, goes in
and out singing songs.

Through the world
I love him, I must be
the moonlight round the door,
round the house in the dark pines.

I shall rise up
with the voice of the birds in the late
year, when their heart,
a hailstone, is white.

The Sarmatian Plain

Soul,
full of darkness, late –
the day with open
pulses, azure –
the plain sings.

Her
song, who
bound to the coast
repeats her swaying song:
sea after storm
her song –

But the towns hear you
– white, quiet
with old sounds –
listen for you on the banks.
Your airs come to them
with a heavy smell
like sand.

And the villages are yours.
The narrow roads run
to you on the greening earth,
on the burnt-out site of your summers
is laid the ashen track
– glass powdered from tears.

There the cattle go,
breathing softly before
the dark. And a child
follows them
piping; the old woman
calls after him
from the fence.

Plain,
gigantic sleep
huge with dreams, your sky
wide, a bell-tower,
the larks high
in the vault –

Rivers along your flanks,
the wet shadows
of the woods, the bright
unending fields,

there the people
whom you preserved
from darkness trod out
their endless time
on the routes of birds
in the early year. I see you:
the heavy beauty
of the blind clay head
– Ischtar or some other name –
found in the mud.

Counterlight

Dusk.
How the grassland
drifts, the wide flood,
plains. Cold, untimely
the moon. A wing-beat now.

Far on the banks
of the rivers,
embraced by
the wide sky,
we heard singing
in the woodshadows. The ancestor
followed overgrown ditches.

Bird-heart, light, feathered
stone on the wind.
Falling
into the mists. Grass and the earth
take you; a trace of
death, a snail's-track long.

But
who will bear me,
the man with closed eyes
and angry mouth, with hands
that hold nothing, who follows
the river, parched;
who in the rain
breathes the other time,
which comes no more, the other,
unspoken, like clouds,
a bird with open wings,
angry, against the sky,
a counterlight, wild.

Pruzzian Elegy

To sing you
one song,
bright with angry love –
but dark, bitter with
grieving, like wet meadow-
herbs, like the bare pines
on the cliff, groaning
beneath the pale dawn wind,
burning before evening –

your never sung
fall, which struck us once
in the blood as our days
of child's-play hung
dream-wide –

then in the forests of the homeland,
above the green sea's
foaming impact, we shuddered
where groves had smoked
with sacrifice, before stones,
by long sunken-in gravemounds,
grass-grown ramparts, under the linden
lightly bent with age –

how rumour hung in its branches!
So in the old women's songs
sounds yet
the scarcely to be fathomed
call of the Foretime –
how we heard then
the echo rotting, the cloudy
discoloured sediment!
So when the deep bells
break, a cracked
tinkle remains.

People of the black woods,
of heavy thrusting rivers,
of empty Haffs, of the sea!
People
of the night-hunt,
of the herds and summer fields!
People
of Perkun and Pikoll,
of the corn-crowned Patrimpe!
People,
like no other, of joy!
People,
like no other, no other, of death! –

People
of smouldering groves,
of burning huts, green corn
trampled, blood-stained rivers –
People,
sacrificed to the singeing
lightning-stroke; your cries veiled
by clouds of flame –
People,
leaping before the strange
god's mother in the throat-
rasping dance
and falling –
how she precedes her
armoured might, rising
above the forest! how the Son's
gallows follows her! –

Names speak of
a stamped-out people, hillsides,
rivers, often still lustreless,
stones and roads –
songs in the evening and legends,
the rustle of lizards names you

and today, like water in the marsh,
a song, poor
with grieving –

poor like the catch of that
white-haired fisherman, always there
on the Haff when the sun
goes down.

Mourning for Jahnn

Voices, loud
across the pumpkin-field,
the road a white smoke,
the wild heads of sunflowers
against noon,
but the voice, one
voice, through
torn lips, crusted blood,
breath of leaves, billowing,
rustling, to be heard:
Come with your small hands,
rue, my mourning-poison, come
as I live I love, I feel
the green fingers, the white
roots, deeper the white roots
drain my heart.

Once the amused gods
called across Tartarus
with lovely voices:
Hang him head down,
then the rock will grow into his mouth.

Villon

You, ranging the landscape
of Touraine: the stony ground
of great cities always
beneath your feet, you
will not return.

Moon
behind you,
long shadows of towers
and trees slanting ahead.
Someone walks there, whistling,
carelessly draped by the
god of thieves, a Greek, they say,
with small shifting
clouds – chiton-weave.

Baldpate, flourish your hat!
Your image on the murderous mirrors
of all the ponds! Far in the windy North
the fishing village:
by the wall, under the sloping
roof, in the mists,
you will sleep, the men
come at morning with the catch, the drink
stands at the back of the hearth,
then the silent martyr leaps
in the pan, glistening with oil,
the fish of the sea – "there I shall sleep".

Góngora

Sword-thrust in the first light!
the Cordovan's line
peels the skin from your heart:
thin, paper, painted
with flying swans.

Oh, the dark cry,
the flight of swans!
To you
a white feather
falls. You shall
write one name with fire
on the sky
– Don Luis' name –
into the silence of the hottest day.

Then down the steps,
in a crowd of boys, comes Lorca.
Oh, Andalusians, children! He sings: Iberia,
black voice, crumbling,
old with the step of kings.
Friends, come in white!
Girls, light, labyrinthine
dance, labyrinthine dance,

Night
or, narrow,
a polished sapphire,
madness, fall on the brow
– as once on Don Luis' brow –
in the midst of sleep!

Günderode

Breath of
prehistory, of ancestral
star-time, rolling suns
over the dance of the peoples,
as the south,
a reddish bird, roars
in the falling mountains.

You
bear
a song on the sword-point,
girl. Voices of birds
in breezes
above the banks now.

But
we see you
clearly, the form of the manly
goddess under the oak-tree,
proud head as
high as the branches.
Dreamily your hands
grasp sleep.

Joseph Conrad

Lines,
on the horizon,
light, colourless hills. The strip
of white. There the flood-tide
reaches its end. The coast
shines fever-green.

And the wind
travels, a leap in the vault
of light, of leaden light. But the ship
is there. I stand here. I have in my lungs
the unending distance.
And speak your name,
my ship.

I look out in the light evening
like the hawk of the hills round Tschernigow;
I hear the white towns and the blossom
on the Dnjestr praised; I call the Polish
carpenter. There,
I say, the boats are black.
I have forgotten that.

Sky above us, distance
darkening up to the sail.
And, in the midst, the burning
fidelity of men, come
across the sea-flood.

Dylan Thomas

Marlais, the clown,
with pouting mouth
he tastes the air. From Ohio
it climbs. And Missouri
comes. The vehement clamour
of his old silence.

Time, built in the wind,
walls of light. Ariadne –
her face depicted against the dusk,
signs, dance
of the bats – labyrinth.

Only in the corner of the eye
the nest,
gray, the coast's bushes, tirelessly
speaking voice
Swansea,
a drowned sailor
who comes down the mist-road.

Marlais,
follow the line of your lashes,
an angry swallow's wing!
before the river
roars, the water rises
round the wall, Babel drowns, the incoherent
speech, the cries, from the battlement
the whisper last of all.

The Singing Swan

Songs of the shepherds
prolonged
on the wave of blood,
he knows you:
the singing swan that rises
yellow-beaked
following the bursting
ice. We hear him darkly,
we met the shepherds,
the birch-winds slept
above the marshes. Our speech
was soft,
a fire,
fallen at nightfall.

Rivers, we shall be
at one with you in the drifting
year, listening on the bed
of summer springs: the singing swan takes wing,
and from Igor's marching army
sounds the sorrowing song,
sung upon towers
in white
breathing air.

Windmill

Light,
foaming light,
over the plain, steep,
mountain of radiance, monstrous
roaring, the storms fly
breathing lightning, the terrible wall
rises in the sky.

I came over the dunes
from the sea
to the treeless riverland,
shadowless, dreamless, I walked
with the reapers, the mill stood
stiff and old. Now with grey
sails it grips the air.
Silent it lifts itself above the land.

It flies off
with the herons, huge
on the white sky. The gleaming eye
of winter watches wildly
in the distance.

Ice-bird heart,
build your nest
of fishbone
and fin in the hollow,
in the whispering blood.
Stay with the children of the plain,
daughters and sons,
stay with the small shadows
of songs and dances,
hold a November grass
against the snow.

Village Road

Guileless the summer:
it goes with the rivers –
hot and cunning:
the roses bloom.
Soon the Scythian frosts,
flaming and within
a stone of smoke, black.

There
from the boundless
sky comes the ploughman
behind his mare, high
in the boughs
of the Ryazan birch
stand the storms, trembling
he sees the shore, the wide
plain sways.

Mikula of the gay mouth,
miraculous ploughman
of wooden Russia, come
to the water-hole and we will sing,
sing strophes made of nothing but wind.
One evening the voice
will sound, Chadayev's voice,
breathing in his despair,
a birdcry.

Roads:
wheeltrack,
hoof-print,
plant
and the dust –
the face of earth
laid on the bed of rivers,

in the sand
which the current drives.
And into my heart. To surface
now no more.

The Church: Comfort My Affliction

Above the walls,
stone, above the arches
the cupolas of wind, joined
beneath the sky, old,
that comes with ferries and rafts,
that sings before dusks
fall, bee-smoke moves with it, breath
of raspberry cane, late –

when the mistress of the fields,
round-eyed, white-haired,
petrifies with slender arms,
light, an ash-tree,
hands of leaf-like cloud,
cups the bitter air
of the marsh and lifts the drink
to her mouth.

On the Tauric Road

This evening: in the wind –
water bears us forth
over the deep –
or half the night
comes on the quail's uneasy
flight, with trembling wings –

Once
on the edge of the steppe,
we came from the cucumber-field,
the camels lay resting
by the road. One
rose, wide-eyed
in its old beauty, looked down the great beasts'
distance, saw the haze
of the Caspian Sea.
Behind that, Enkidu:

as he approached
from the gazelles' water-hole
with glowering face. I was born on the steppe,
he says, I shall fight
in the cedar-wood.

Landscape with Birds

Old, plains of last year's
grass, greater, the hills
all sunk. The lake
white, stretching past the horizon.
From there the crane. High.
Above the light. Following
its own shadow.

And a voice
like a grove and full of green
shadows, wet, when the water
recedes. Lark, the stone
burst on which you sang
morning after morning
before the leather tent.
Only one man heard you
Temujin, waking,
heard you.

Once, having slept
an eternity, walled up,
they broke open the cave, seven men
stepped out. A tree
has grown round me, with hard
bark, like sleep, the raven
preens its plumage in the branches
overhead. My tree,
trembling, where my heart beats
against you, winterly, but
your bark will not burst.

Even if the snow
should powder
as the raven
moves its wing.

Steppe

There was one
who sang into evening. Outside
the heavy plain,
treeless, sand burning
around the low brush –
then the clouds hung dark
and a moon hung down.
The dun-coloured herd
at the water-hole. A man,
brown-bearded, came and drove
the cattle away. In the window
the other man sang.

Villages,
how shall I go on
living? I know in the distance
the splendour of endlessly running
skies. I heard the boy
who sang and the herdsman
with the bright eyes talking
by the roadside, I stood,
the village at my back.

Lake Ilmen 1941

Wilderness. Against the wind.
Numb. The river sunk
into the sand.
Charred branches:
the village before the clearing. Then
we saw the lake –

– Days of the lake. Of light.
A track in the grass,
the white tower stands
like a gravestone
deserted by the dead.
The broken roof
in the caw of crows.
– Nights of the lake. The forest
falls into the marshes.
The old wolf,
fat from the burnt-out site,
startled by a phantom.
– Years of the lake. The armoured
flood. The climbing darkness
of the waters. One day
it will strike
the storming birds from the sky.

Did you see the sail? Fire
stood in the distance. The
wolf crossed the clearing.
Listens for the bells of winter.
Howls for the enormous
cloud of snow.

River Poem

Dream,
sudden,
from fires of the hawk's night,
flash, animal eye,
under unblinking lid,
reeds, quiver of arrows,
where the otter, a heart-leap,
plunges.

Before the gleam,
the white
wall of light,
before the climbing
horizon, lit by cries,
lifted from the deep,
over the darkness,
the restless animal heart,
feeding and spawning,

steps the river,
it comes
weaponless, another
hero who devoured his childhood,
now it is the wood
it eats and follows

to the hill,
to the blackness
– the calamus in the sword–dance
shines before the day –
into the dark of the fens

as far as the haze–land: islands,
floating, morass, fallen
gates, sunken
arches, flags of birdbone

and seaweed –
it dies on the slime,
gulls cover the bubble of breath
in the shallows.

Dream,
ending with the hawk's
cry, with the high
roar,
signs on a bluish wall
scratched in the plaster
with a fingernail, vision,
image,
Sarmatian,

long
I follow you
river,
at the edges of woods,
tiring
easily, a sound
in old pewter.

The Homeland of the Painter Chagall

Still round the houses
the dry scent of the woods,
cranberry and club-moss.
And the evening cloud
sinking around Vitebsk, sounding
from its own darkness. Within it
a thin laugh, as the old man
peeped from the roof
at the wedding-feast.

And we hung in dreams.
But assurance ringed
the stars of our fathers' home,
bearded, like angels, and with trembling mouth,
with wings of cornfields:

Nearness of futurity, this
burning bugle-call;
as it darkens, the town
swims through the clouds,
red.

Latvian Songs

My father the hawk.
Grandfather the wolf.
And my forefather the rapacious fish in the sea.

I, unbearded, a fool,
lurching against the fences,
my black hands strangling a lamb
in the early light. I,

who beat the animals
instead of the white
master, I follow the rattling caravans
on washed-out roads,

I pass through the glances
of the gipsy women. Then
on the Baltic shore I meet Uexküll, the master.
He walks beneath the moon.

Behind him, the darkness speaks.

The Duna

Duna, dawn
and the splendid wind
of the plains always about you.
The old town lies in the smoke.

Cold your banks. Bushes,
a green strip. Your swallows
swoop into
the light.

Weary
at noon
I have come,
I fall on the sand.
I will live from the breath
of the rivers, drink
from the springs, the waters
of earth and night, from secret depths
under the grass.

I will live in the fire
of day, part the flames
to see you: in the climbing year
you walk with a heavy mouth,
dark – the gulls
and the waters flash,
screaming the sea receives you –
you move towards it.

In its shadow,
from the deep
the old creatures
sigh to you.

Nightway

Easy
to watch the stars,
old images: Bull and
Swan and the Wagoner, –
were I a bush in the night,
a tendril, black with dew, curled round
my lady Dryas –
easy
to sing the song of the mist.

But the moon, an old
transparent metal – no one knows now –
sounds to the armies of birds,
to the calling migrant wedge
above. Or perhaps
to the dancers of midnight.

Once our ancestor saw them
above the valley-brink:
slender, with pointed steps. In the field-wind I
heard screams as from plunging
chariots, the hounds
raced past, ahead of the rider.
I listened by the willow
the way the hunters went.

Kaunas 1941

Town,
branches over the river,
copper-coloured, like branching candles.
The banks call from the deep.
Then the lame girl
walked before dusk,
her skirt of darkest red.

And I know the steps,
the slope, this house. There is no
fire. Under this roof
lives the Jewess, lives whispering
in the Jews' silence
– the faces of the daughters
a white water. Noisily
the murderers pass the gate. We walk
softly, in musty air, in the track of wolves.

At evening we looked out
over a stony valley. The hawk
swept round the broad dome.
We saw the old town, house after house
running down to the river.

Will you walk over
the hill? The grey processions
– old men and sometimes boys –
die there. They walk
up the slope ahead of the slavering wolves.

Did my eyes avoid yours
brother? Sleep struck us
at the bloody wall. So we went on
blind to everything. We looked
like gipsies at the villages

in the oak-wood, the summer
snow on the roofs.

I shall walk on the stone banks
under the rainy bushes,
listen in the haze of the plains.
There were swallows upstream
and the woodpigeon called
in the green night:
My dark is already come.

The Hawk

"Wing,
bird-wing,
arch in the smoke, light –
fall out of sleep,
arrow, sweep over the
river, fly, a strip of rain,
in the light of the banks."

Water-haze, white,
which darkens
the feather. Wind,
which roughens me. Storm
across the plains. Crumbling with weeds,
evening, water-bushes.

"Under the drag of the air
outside dreamless he travels
with staring eyes, the killer
travels with the wind."

Oh, borne up
over the tree
of dusk, high in the light,
the rushing silence – yet still
light, sea, wave-song, the sails
over the depth, upon the seaweeds'
shadow, I travel through the light –
travel with the storm,
higher, he hunts with the scourge,
night-storm, the cutting knife of luck
between his teeth.

Return

Bench, a hard meuble.
There, between pine-trees,
the swing – a board, two rough
poles. Cuckoo,
blue roller and hoopoe;
the nightingale, thrush–nightingale,
sings shorter, laconically,
huskier, God willing.

But I came to sleep
under the log-wall,
sleep of gossamer and toad's gold,
fly-legged sleep. The light
recedes. Cows plod
in their own shadows. The fish
strikes a foaming line
across the water.

But I only sleep.
I am not here.
I seek a place,
only a grave wide, the little hill
over the meadows. From there
I can see
the river.

Fire and Snow

Fire,
the birchwood
burns, from the black waves,
from the billow
of smoke
leaps the flame,
the wild dance of flame, allurement
seizes the skin, allurement
of flame.

In the sea
is a road, a great
animal eye, weeping and wide
open, the green lash
over the cheek of salt,
coolness, allurement
of coolness.

Both
– the young man –
allurement of flame, allurement
of coolness, the dance
over the cloud, the coolness
of salt or snow, the young
man in the first hour
of day, lovely with exhaustion,
his head built of
shadows.

In my breath,
fire and snow, I live.
So you come in the fire,
so you come tomorrow
in snow.

Lake Shore

What still lives
in the quicksand
under the fin-wings
of the great fish –
dwindling green, algae, a sea-moss
which clings to the moon,
at morning, when she drowns –

is like a word unsaid,
heard in the hollow of the mouth,
in the quiver of the temple,
in the hair. We drift to the bank,
with bluish hands my love,
white.

Come,
it is cold, the straw
will hear us, the coverlet
over the sigh, the creaking
wall of wood. Sleep, a whisper,
lies down with us.

One Day

One day we shall have
both hands full of light –
the strophes of night, the moving
waters meeting the banks
again, the rough eyeless
sleep of the beasts in the reeds
after the embrace – then
we shall stand against the slope,
outside, against the white
sky which comes cold
over the hill, the cascade of radiance,
and is frozen, ice,
as if fallen from stars.

I want to rest for that
little while upon your brow,
forgetful, letting
my blood wander silent
through your heart.

The Memel

Beyond the fields, far,
beyond the meadows,
the river.
From its breath
the night rises.
The bird crosses the hill
and cries.

Once we went
with the wind, fixed the net
at the mouth of the meadowbrook.
A lantern hung
in the alders. The old man
took it down.
The smugglers' boat ground on the sand.

Out of the darkness
you come, my river,
out of the clouds.
Roads run down to you
and the rivers, Jura and Mitva,
young, from the woods, and loamy
Szeszupe. With poles the loggers
drift by. The ferry
lies on the sand.

And the sky
dark with migrating birds.
In the air of beating wings, high,
reed-sound, well-smoke, smoke of resinous woods.
By the birches above the bank now
the women stand with red
and yellow ribbons – one
draws her daughters
to her swollen belly, the young
sons bathe in the river.

River,
alone always
can I love you
only.
Image of silence.
Plaques for the future: my cry.
Which never held you.
Now in the dark
I hold you fast.

The Daubas

Above beat the wind.
We lived in the huts on the river.
The sound of reeds
darkened the banks.

We were children in our
hearts which sang us through the years.
In the manner of earth
came frosts and rain,
lightning and clouds, like the time –

like the time
that we took
and gave from hands
red with fruit. The winters
flowed into the light.

That is gone.
We left the villages to the sand.
With less than a logger's cry
we came away.

Following bitterness we lay
wood to foreign fires,
know one song yet: once
the apple-tree bloomed.

Where then
do we want to abide?
It is always the earth,
the ground where we shall lie.
The children
will not find the village.

But the gardens, the strip of reeds
at the river – that riverland Daubas –
yellowing barns –
and the horse-team which came from the wood –
the hawk in the empty blue –

these still stain our sight.
So we step under the arch
of these years. And add
our joys to the earth.

Feeling the blood in the temples,
as you stroke your daughters' hair,
at evening you speak: Come,
dearest, you are still here – so
that I do not yearn.

Winterlight

In this night
I listen long for you
distant rivers, your first
ice. I hear
that small sound of rushes;
the village sleeps.

Childhood, sepia, a cold
well-water, sandy –
the wooden bucket always
swung down. Who came?
who loosened the rusty chain?
ah, who drank?

The dark speaking kindness
of our huts, their soft
word is snowed-in,
old aunts' whispers, children's cries –

That time of lilac-colour
when birds hung in the moving
sky, in the vanishing
light; the sky
stood still,
halted above the barn roof,
silent, drew in the shadows.

Winter always came.
The blue deepened
with pigeons' wings, a sloping
roof, a soft shimmer
over the world.

And the hunter's cry leapt
on the slope, towards the
quiet snow. O deep
blackness! your heart
full of light!

Recall

Fire,
the temptation in the blood:
the comely man. What has passed
is like sleep, dreams
along rivers,
on the waters,
without sail, in the current.

Plains – the lost
villages, the forests' edge.
And a thin smoke
in the air,
straight.

Once,
blubber-lipped, Perkun
came, a feather in his beard,
came in the track of the elk,
the Stutterer came,
travelled the river, drew
darkness, a fishing-net, after him.

There
I was. In the old time.
What is new has never begun. I am a man,
of one flesh with his wife,
who raises his children
for an age without fear.

from *Shadowland Rivers*

The Call of the Quail

Out of the flying darkness,
deep,
before the waters'
sound, rain
or the stream,
late for me, a man
who plans to sharpen the scythe,

quail, I loved to hear
your call,
simply, it moved
before the dusk, "God be
praised" or "I fly forth", I walk
over the hill, I push
off from the bank, I reach
the willows, I step
over the threshold,

"God be praised"
I say and spend
the night without the return
of a dream,
which I recognize
by a light like salt,
broken and bluish:

rows of poplar, the carriage
on the Gronow highway,
Pan Thadeusz lets
fall a glove
and steps on it, and the horses
rear their heads, once
the Pole laid his lance
by the pricked-up
ear of his steed,

across the Yenisei
river
the stones speak, the stony women
with round mouths
across the steppe, from the stream
Zbruch the four-faced
wood-poles, across the kurgans
cry the birds, Laima
sits, a goddess, in the open
belfry, on the white
stone pedestal.

Here
at the stone
which weights the field
I would echo
a cricket, on the stony ground,
I would enter a house,
blackish, of wood, with high-pitched
roofs, a tent, raised for horsemen,
erected above red
images, the gold and great
faces, above
the crosses, but eternally
in mists, before the rain
drives down, the stream
sounds, I loved to hear
"I fly forth" called
simply in the darkness into
the wave of silence, which swells,
the depths behind it, spaceless,
void, I heard
from the darkness
"God be praised".

The Eagle

With wings spread wide
over the river
over the wood in the marsh
the eagle hovers – a sign
with smouldering edges
in the arch of air,
talons gouged into the wood
of my door – I shall
awaken, bemused, on the wooded hill
awaken with startled eyes
in the bushes.

I have nailed the eagle
with outspread wings
on the ridge of my house – I shall
sleep, fly in
sleep – an ashen portent –
over the woods.

Plain

Lake.
The lake.
Sunken
the banks. Under the cloud
the crane. White, lighting up
nomadic
ages. With the wind

I came up the hill.
Here I shall live. I was
a hunter, but the grass
caught me.

Teach me to speak, grass,
teach me to be dead and listen,
long, and speak, stone,
teach me to stay, water
go on, and wind, without me.

Calls

Above the broad slope –
the meadow, the fences, above
the poles – I was the wind
and unceasing speech
of the river below, I came with
hands of calamus, I was
without sound, I lay
in the grass with opened temples,
the crickets bound
my hair.

One, always, who
takes me up, he has
flown above the winds, he has
listened to the speech
in the sand of the shore, where the cold
burns, hoarfrost formed
on your eye, silent ice
of a flower, a tear
at noon.

He has heard me. I did not see
the man who lowered
the rod, the women
rinsed the washing from the boat,
the other man with horses
came along the towpath, in the smoke
above the fences the song
of two calls rose, one
sounded light and the answer
deep, but at evening
were caught in the wind.

Dryad

Birch, cool
with sap, tree, your breath
in my hands, tense
bark, a yielding glass,
but to feel deeper
stirrings, the stretching
in the trunk,
towards the branches.

Let
your hair fall,
fall in your neck, I hear
with my hands, I hear
through the coolness, I hear a fluttering,
hear the current lift,
the rising flood,
hear ecstasy
sing in my ear.

At the River

Sky,
the blue, old
arch, which goes with
us, which the green
enchants: bank, the lovely
tree, its shadow which
moves on the water.

There is a strip of red,
a trace
of red, we are that red alone
between green and blue,
sky and earth,
when did you say:

"The shadows fly, a
night has called
with owlet voices which came
near under the trees,
the sky was gone"?

Now,
the sky is new,
breath, and no blue,
your temple rests (a slow
beat, no more to be heard,
never more) upon my mouth.

Summer Cries

Peewit,
fly forth round
the crest of my day,
over the short
horn, fly down the
pasture on lurching
wings, fly off into the
fens.

Wide, so that I drown,
body, breathing, I stand
with lifted arms, I have
waited, I clutch at a cloud, I have
called, I hear that call, far –

where I stood with lifted
arms, I ruffled
a cloud.

Unsaid

Heavy,
I grow down,
I spread roots
in the ground,
the waters of earth
find me, rise,
I taste bitterness – you
are without earth,
a bird of the air, lighter
always in light,
only my fear still
holds you
in the earthly wind.

Tale

Bright sand, tracks,
green, and the flying wood
darkness, high the steel fish
soars through the trees,
up over the tops, I
take only a step,
and another step.

Kitesh, the town,
has towers
and a street,
there I stand,

eyeless I see you,
I step towards you
unheard,
I speak to you
without a voice.

The Wanderer

Evening,
the river sounds,
the heavy breath of the woods,
sky full of
shrieking birds, coasts
of darkness, old,
above the fire of stars.

Human have I lived,
forgetting to count
the open doors. I have knocked
at the closed doors.

Every door is open.
The host stands with outspread
arms. Come to the table.
Speak: The woods sound,
the fish fly through the
breathing river, the sky
trembles with fires.

The Animals at Christmas

I am in a rage, says the cock,
I want my idyll.
Then save your comb my dear, I say,
for now the hens lose their feathers.
Ah, I just sing, he says,
and I in the early dusk
go round the house, round the wood
the badger
draws his staggering track.

And no snow.
Only the owl
with cat–like sounds. The firs
damp. The light trembles
on the mists.

We shall
scatter straw. Assemble
the silence under the roof,
open the windows once
for a candle-dance,
bring gifts to ox and ass,
we know a story
which is as we are – a great
darkness under the heavens
in which the winters drive
with red wings, haloed
by silver voices.

Winter Cries

Crows, crows,
green ice, crows
over the river. Frozen
bushes march
up the bank.

The snow does not
powder when brushed by your
wing, bird, bush-bird, but
a little blood
your heart
in ice, your call
a wisp of smoke over
the sandbank,

where embraces were
untiring the river
has always lived.

The Death of the Wolf

Between wood and river –
but it is
night, in the moonlight
wolves, the long shadows,
gone. But my boar comes,
stout-hearted, a peasant
eager to reap
his field.

Autumn,
melt away with the
mists! Now a dark season
crouches before the high
wall, before the ice,
the owls swoop over the snow
spitting at dusk,
a sail of sleep,
lost.

But broken. There were
tracks on the road from
the farm. I came with
an axe on my shoulder.
Near the drift
lay the wolf, disembowelled,
its flank savaged.

Pig, I say, brave
little pig, you have put paid
to that devil. I am glad
to hear your snorting,
it makes me warm
in the dark.

Hamann

That
one world,
roads, ways, today
Wasianski is coming – who
wrote the Lives
and who the poems à la Grécourt,
between Lizentgraben and
Katzbach the whole, what do I know, world.

But a bird sings
through the night, in the
too heavily pruned trees,
summerlong this bird,
it does not wake my son,
but I – so I shall
go, I fish for a dish of
will-o'-the-wisp in the meadows
behind the ditch.

World. I see in the rain
a white cloud. It is I.
Down the Pregel
the boat. From the mists. World.
A hell, in which God dwells.
World. I say with Sancho:
God, I say: he understands me.

Elder-Blossom

Here comes
Babel, Isaak.
He says: In the pogrom
when I was a child
they tore the head
off my pigeon.

Houses in a wooden street,
at the fences, elder.
Down the small steps
the white-scrubbed threshold –
then, you remember,
the flecks of blood.

People, you say: Forget it –
there are young people coming,
their laughter like elder-bushes.
People, the elder
might die
of your forgetfulness.

To the Chassid Barkan

You came as we were singing,
gave greeting, watched
the swallows. In the midday
shadows we listened to the sighs
and curses of the old men.

You came over
the hill. So your men
always came, armoured
with beards and names, but
prayer-curl and feet
flying free in the dance, from burning
thorn-bush, from a river
(on the willows hung the harps).

Do not go. The time
will come to love your ways,
to know the deep darkness
of woods and rivers,
to sow in tears,
to reap in joy.

Memorial Leaf

Years,
gossamer,
the great spiders, years –
the gipsies with horses
travelled the dirt road. The old gipsy
came with the whip, the women
stood at the farm gate talking,
in cradling arms
the handful of luck.

Later they came no more.
Then the stranglers came with leaden
eyes. Once the old woman
in the attic
asked about those who had vanished.

Hear the rain streaming
down the slope, they walk,
who will not be seen again,
down the old dirt road,
wrapped in the spuming
waters, wind–crowns of alien lands
resting lightly
on their black hair.

Weathersigns

With the stream,
down the meadow-stream,
with the wild smell
of the woods, talking
aloud with the summer light

and the birds
towards evening, with the bats
in the dark – zigzagging
they flew up and down
round a barn with little
dragon's wings – talking
I came here, here I am,

on the sand-hill, I set my foot
into the dry moss, I have borne the broad
sky, the breathing airs, I stagger,
there is a roar, I listen
in the drumming darkness,

listen to the stream, it lay
on the sand, the wind
guided its hands,
the summer came

with lassitudes, with
blood in the eyes, pounding
temples, the mouth full of rust,

but it guided the hands
of my stream, which goes towards
the fires in the shadow of fish,
in the shadow of reeds,
in the shadow of trees –

flame, fly, the coasts
turn in on the land,
soundless, blowing from dunes,
the stones sink around
the forsaken sea – fire,
set your wings like smoke
into the tempest, it bears you before the
storms, before the raging silence,

before the skies break,
the boiling storms, broken
the airs then, motionless on the sand
the stream

and the hill struck,
I hold a tree, I am still talking:
We saw the signs come
and go, two feathers
fell down through the silence.

Lament

Voices, the wind
comes across
the bay, reedwork, Elsinore
sounded thus: over the straits
the coast, stretched
against the sky, there
on the headland stands
he who has called me,
Helios, broad-mouthed,
dark under the
eyebrows – the fires round him,
round shoulder and hair, the clanging
trains, uproarious: Planets,
the murderous
concentus of the world.

Over the bay,
far,
over the rain,
out of mists, shining with colours,
the rainbow – peace
is promised us.

Sea-Piece

Stay,
gullcry,
when the sun declined –
the swallow which we loved
came then no more.
Deep, riddled with hail,
the winter,
old.

Did you stay,
a friend with gentle speech,
with easy
hands? – we heard the drag
of air and the dusk, I have
drunk a water.

Soon,
with burning sails,
I shall go, Boötes to my right,
above my head the Swan, –
windless, night, I shall go,
a phantom.

French Village

Martin,
in a cloud
of white momentous birds
the saint comes, and the year,
under the hardy maple the year
goes out.

When it darkens,
the singing silence
lives, a speaking water, a half cry
behind the house with the sign,
the wind-blown converse of shepherds.

Ah, when the year
darkens, when I see the weathercock
spin, and tell the time by that –
hoist, Angélique, the summer,
the red skirt, out of the highest
window cry me into the light.

Brentano in Aschaffenburg

Signs.
A peach-tree
twisted on the trellis
under the wall. So the stone
crumbles brighter.

Ah a leaf
against the red here:
wall, church and summer-house.
Stairs. Down the street.
Outside the meadows.

Cool. Airs of green.
The river embedded before
the open sky. The howl
in the falling wind.

———

"Woe, without sacrifice . . . "
The dust on the staircase
reddish, a man comes,
fat, his hand on his heart,
he unlocks the oaken door.

Hölderlin in Tübingen

Trees, earthly, and light
in which the boat stands, called,
the oar against the bank, the lovely
slope, before this door
walked the shadow which has
fallen upon a river
Neckar, which was green, Neckar,
winding through
meadows and willows.

Tower,
that it be dwelt in
like a day, the walls'
weight, the weight
against the green,
trees and water, to weigh
both in one hand:
the bell sounds down
over the roofs, the clock
moves to the turn
of the weathervane.

Night-Swallows

I

Cold,
the pierced air,
the black and the white, light, speaking
on routes of birds. The evening, its bull-horn
aslant in the fire-smoke on the horizon. You saw
the fish rise, as the waters
clashed, you took your hand
from my eyes, blackness flew
round us and without wing
and without cry.

II

We breathed,
the roof on my shoulder
was light and like a rain
skyless
the needles strewn in the sand,
night-swallows, souls,
where shadow was,
thick on the earth,
cold.

From the Rivers

Ce n'était pas assez que tant de mers,
ce n'était pas assez que tant de terres
eussent dispersé la course de nos ans.

ST.-JOHN PERSE

Come from the rivers
of the sea, gone
through teeth and claws, surf,
coasts, these woods of trembling air –
raised is
the high plain
with wrinkled hide, brownish
with fissures, cliffs of fall – here
time is a cloud,
immense, climbing across
the sky and drinking
the pure airs, breathing
the rains of light.

Islands always, you know that,
across the waters, across
the distance, there you were born,
wavering, there you were born,
at a time which was a bird
feathered with countless
colours between
ochre and rose, it was
a bird, you know.

But you stood before the plain
you have climbed
the mountains behind the bearers, you
stood before sleep, before the plain,
which awoke beneath white
lids to a green beast's
singing, the dweller
in flying woods, unaware
of its wings.

There
live! your eyes scan
the sea, a current,
white, still white when it
darkens, without vehemence, laid
close under the heart,
speaking, darkness, the
sails of voices, held
by red–haired men
in feathered cloaks, at evening

under the wind.

Bird Routes 1957

I

I slept in the rain,
I woke in rainy reeds.
Before the leaves fall, I see the moon near,
I hear the cry of migrating birds,
the shaker of air, the white
cry, which shatters the air.

Swift and sharp
as the scenting wolves,
sister, listen! Väinemöinen
sings through the wind,
throws a pinion of snow
round your shoulder, we drift
winged in a wind of songs –

II

but under great
skies alone, deserted
streets of the feathered
armies, which have passed –
sleeping on the winds
they went, a new
sun flamed, the blaze
leapt up, they burned
in the ash tree.

There our songs
also took wing.
Sister, your hands
bleach, you sleep on in
darkness – when shall I
sing of the birds' fear.

Gertrud Kolmar

Beech, bloody in leaf,
in smoking depth, bitter
the shadows, the door above
of shouting magpies.

There a girl walked,
a girl with smooth hair,
the plain under her lids
glanced up, her step
was lost in the marshes.

But the dark time
is not dead, my speech
wanders and is
rusty with blood.

Were I to remember you:
I stepped in front of the beech,
I have commanded the magpie:
Be silent, they come, who were
here – if I remembered:
We shall not die, we shall
be girded about with towers.

Else Lasker-Schüler

I strew
wind–broken branches
over the earth. Sister. Each
undying land
is your grave.

Przemysl, Brzozow, who
scratched out
his grave
sprawls in it. In Mielce the house
of god
burning, the voice rising
over the flames, one
voice, but
from a hundred mouths, out
of the suffocation. How does
one say: in the furnace
rose the praise
of God – how does
one say?

I know
no more.
Over the earth, sister,
wind–broken branches, scattered.
Like trees clutching
at what was seen in
the midday shadow, in
the dusk under the wings
of the birds, in
the ice, in
the waste
of night.

Love
(you speak from the grave)

Love steps, a white
figure,
from the middle of horror.

To Nelly Sachs

> "The foxes have holes, and the birds
> of the air have nests"

Holes the foxes
run down,
and the wood-pole Perun,
which was scorched and swamped,
is also gone
into the earth, beneath
the Dnieper, its speech
still cries from the river: Come
from broken groves, come
beasts, the foxes have holes.

Who bears the skies,
stands over
towers of light, his
is the tree, his brood
under the wings, shadow
feeds him and rain, the birds,
the hastening hearts,
have a nest.

(High, a flash, the eagle
soared, in its talons
the screaming nightingale, the swallows called
over the burned-out site –
the man in the hole
fell on the earth wall, he
smeared sand on his brow,
the roots ate
sight and hearing.)

Who hath, that he lay
his head, he will
sleep, hear from dreams
into a cry which flies
over the plains, flies over
waters – a light came, parted
two hills, perceptible
the path, the stones, banks,
green with lustre – the soundless
cry, "Dandelion seeds,

but winged with prayers".

The Don

High, the villages
of fire. The banks fall
across rock. But
the river imprisoned, it breathed
ice, dark silence
followed it.

The river was white. The higher
bank dark. The horses
climbed up the slope. Once
the banks opposite
fell away, we saw,
behind the fields, far,
under the early moon, walls
against the sky.

There
the Div sings
in the tower,
he cries at the cloud, the bird
of only ill–omen, he calls
over the rocky banks,
commands the plains to hear.
Hills, open up, he says,
step out in armour you dead,
put on the helmet.

Ikons

Towers, arched, fenced
with crosses, red. The sky
breathes darkly, Joann
stands on the hill, the town
against the river. He watches
the sea come with planks,
oars, scabbed
fishes, the wood
throws itself down in the sand.
Before the wind
walks the prince, brandishing
torches in either hand he strews
silent fires
over the plains.

Deserted Township

Across the empty
market-place the wind,
a chicken's-wing,
draws a track in the dust.

Fences. Lopsided
crosses. Jackdaw-voice.
Who comes, a board on his shoulder,
who will cut a new sill
for the window, who
came, a green pot
under the shawl?

Here no one comes. The sky
finds a ribbon
lying and whisks it up,
moss grows on the
housewall, mist flies
round a white tower, and where
have you come from?

Across the moaning fences
of the pastures, across
the meadow near the bog-hole,
black water follows you, drowning your footprints.

Under the Edge of Night

Under the edge of night the small
towns in the wind, a jumble
of roofs, yellowing walls
and towers. The land engulfs them.

Tents, frayed with the echo
of dead voices, torn mouths of bells,
tents with laced flaps, freezing
with age against the sky.

And the plain runs
through their streets, pauses
in the squares before open
doors and above the wells.

But in the nights: they travel
down rivers, sails in the stiff
forest of masts, sails,
wet, painted, peeling
flags. I came

under the edge of night, squatting
outside, before the wood
began, a village, like the
swarthy gipsy woman, in the glow
she swung the small pan over
the dying fire, the smoke
parted her hair.

North Russian Town

(PUSTOSHKA 1941)

Pale
by the road to the North
falls the mountain-wall. The bridge,
the old wood,
the bushy banks.

There the stream lives,
white in the pebbles, blind over the
sand. And the caw of crows
speaks your name: Wind
in the rafters, a smoke
towards the evening.

It comes,
glowing in
the cloud, it follows the winds,
it watches for the fire.

Remote fire breaks forth
in the plain,
far. Who dwell near
forests, on streams, in the wooden
luck of the villages, listen
at evening, lay
an ear to the earth.

In Transit

No one will learn where we were,
dogs with dull eyes
saw us run down
past the fences, black the house
and hilly the land round the source
of the Volga, house and wall,
faded the image:

Tolstoy, old, erect on the planks
of the wooden railway station,
boorish with frightening
hands, which are too thin
for discourse in the castle of intellect,

where the shadow drags past
the fences – I do not know
the graves, but I know
he rose from the vaults,
I lean back in the light, which falls
on the mountains with wildness of air –
flights of birds, cries
behind me, above me,
in the distance – I stood
on buried streams,
heard the sand sigh,
I was a wooden shadow,
banded with iron, bounded
by falling light.

Above the River

Sand,
cold, lively
with springs, silent in the breath
of the river it goes, following the current
through the lake, over
the open eye of the deep,
over sleep
like a light, gleaming
with fins, in the mists
the birds follow it.

Then
the shore again
receives it with green
hands, with the dark earth
and the beasts which show their backs.

But the town
comes, curved white
on the banks, resounding with towers,
with walls in the crow's shadow
toward evening, with gold
above the ridges, the town,
soft with the din of its childhood,
with stinging frosts, with age,
with the snow outside.

Snow, which fills
the sky, and the void
behind the red, behind the fires,
the void. Wind, you fly
with the birds, fall down
over my sail, I call you,
wind, I see the plains
averted, old.

Cathedral 1941

Which we saw
across the winter river,
across the black torrent
of the waters, Sophia, sounding
heart of benighted Novgorod.

Once before it was dark.
But a time came,
passing with gay foaming
dolphins, orchards
burnt your cheek, often
behind your fences pilgrims
halted, wet-faced,
in your cupolas' golden cry.

And your night, the moon-abyss,
deathly pale, the halcyon bird
glittered in the icy nest.

Smoke has blackened
your walls, fire broke
your doors, how shall the light
be for your window-sockets.
All was done to our
life, the cry as well
as the silence, we saw
your face, white,
rising over the plains.

Then wrath sprang up
outside
in the marshes.
Wrath, a heavy seed.
How shall I call
one day
my eye still
bright?

Village Church 1942

Smoke
around log-wall and snowy roof.
Tracks of crows
down the slope. But the river
in the ice.

There
dazzle, broken
stone, debris, the arch,
sundered the wall,

where the village stood
against the hill, the river
sprang in the early year,
a lamb, before the door,
a round bay
lay open to the wind,

which blows round the heights,
sombre, its own
shadow, it calls, rough-voiced
the crow
cries back.

Report

Bajla Gelblung,
escaped in Warsaw
from a transport from the Ghetto,
the girl took to the woods,
armed, was picked up
as partisan
in Brest-Litovsk,
wore a military coat (Polish),
was interrogated by German
officers, there is
a photo, the officers are young
chaps, faultlessly uniformed,
with faultless faces,
their bearing
is unexceptionable.

Cloister Near Novgorod

River, heavy,
where the air sags, old,
ghosts of the deep
plain, speaking in rain
down the banks. The pike
lies under the reeds.

Light on the white wall
like a tolling bell,
the starve-cloth night
sinking over the roofs, transpierced
by silenced birds.

Doors, empty, the stony
path, on the overgrown step
the old man with the white head,
when song rises in the resounding
arch, wind steps through the armoured
door, the pike rises,
silvery,
rigid-finned, to the surface.

The Tomsk Road

A cry, the wind
strikes at the harpchords
– entrails, wound on branches
of the birch, there
runs the ridge of hills,
I hear a harp behind
the embankment, but I
do not see the road, Yelisaveta
said once:

On the road to Tomsk
the peasants at night
put kvass and bread in the window,
the stranger came,
passed by, no one
said "Exile", he was
"unlucky", he had
a hundred names, any
could call him.

That was the road, said
Yelisaveta, it ran
in a land like the sky,
in a summer foaming
with flowers, the giant trees
bore the sky, but
snow came, Yelisaveta
came years after,
her brothers stood on the bank
her grandson stepped on to the road,
threw the fishing-rod into the grass.

Easter

There yet the hills,
the darkness, but
the ascent is good, the plains
approach from the distance, their cry
comes with the wind.

Over the wood. The river
comes, the birchwoods
grow up to the wall, towers,
stars round the cupolas, the golden
roof lifts a cross on chains.

Then,
in the sombre silence,
light, singing, at first
as from under the earth, bells, tolling,
the cock-crow of voices

and embrace of the air,
resounding air, towers
on a white wall, the high
towers of light, I have
your eyes, I have your cheek,
I have your mouth, the Lord
is risen, so call,
eyes, call, cheek, call, mouth,
cry Hosanna!

Russian Songs

Marina
singing down
from a tower across a landscape
of rocks, three rivers
beneath her feet, but
night and the shadows
of wind in flight.

Beautiful lover,
my tree,
high in your branches
with brow bared
to the moon
I sleep, buried
in my wings.

I sleep –
you give me a grain of salt
scooped from an uncrossed
sea, I give you
a drop of rain
from the land
where no one weeps.

In Memory of B.L.

When the village
sounds, breathing green
around sand-track and fence,
when it has rained,
swallow-flight, sky,
white, big enough for a rainbow,
evening, the hand
which cradles the brow, the mouth
sings without sound.

And nothing
more to be called.
There fly the stars with roaring
wings, your death
questions my life. Rain
(I say) and green, the bird
brushed the rainbow,
light powdered, a blazing
cloud, we saw him
no more.

The Ford

Your white roads wound
through the woods at noon.
One led down the green slope
to the river,
drank from the water of the ford.
The swallow flew up.

And I know the hut
across in the cherry-trees. There
you walked. Reed flutes
sounded. In the snow,
in the windfall,
I shall return.

Log-Cabin

Young
then the house,
of white pine –
lively with flowing sap,
talking the night through,
beams and boards circled
by dreams, winged, soft
under the pines, soundless
the owls flew.

Without bark
in the storms
you stood, in long rains,
frosts clawed
into your door. So old, you
move me to tears. Thus we
all return, we carry
our dead beneath your roof.

You with the moon
and the winds of summer lift
up your face, it is bright –
thus from the girls' faces
shines the hard beauty of love.

House,
one day, when you die,
all will fall,
walls and roof and hearth
will fall, so love
falls – its rustle, how it darkens,
and the place thereof
shall know it no more.

Village Music

Final boat in which I fare
hat no more upon my hair
in four oak-boards smooth and white
rue-sprig in my hand held tight
my friends walk, I ride in state
   someone blows the trumpet
   someone the trombone
boat don't sink beneath my weight
hear the others talking grand:
"this bloke built upon the sand"

From the branchless tree the crow
perched upon the top cries: "Woe"
from the well-pole tall and trim:
"take the parting gift from him
"take that sprig of rue away"
   but there blares the trumpet
   there blares the trombone
no one has removed the spray
all say: "now he's gone although
"out of time's not far to go"

Now I know it and I fare
hat no more upon my hair
moonlight round my beard and brow
too far gone for fooling now
listen as I lie below
   up there sounds the trumpet
   up there the trombone
in the distance calls the crow
I am where I am: in sand
with the rue-sprig in my hand.

The Road Home

Blue.
The air.
The high tree
round which the heron flies.
And the house,
once, where now the wood
grows down,
small and white
the house, and the green shimmer,
a willow leaf.

Wind. It has led me.
I lay before the threshold.
The wind has covered me. To where
should I have followed it? I have
no wings. At evening
I threw
my cap to the birds.

Dusk. The bats
swoop round my head. The oar
broken, so I shall not sink, I walk
on the water.

Always to be Named

Always to be named:
the tree, the bird in flight,
the reddish rock where the river
flows, green, and the fish
in white smoke, when darkness
falls over the woods.

Signs, colours, it is
a game, I think
it may not end
well.

And who will teach me
what I forgot: the stones'
sleep, the sleep
of the birds in flight, the trees'
sleep, their speech
moves in the darkness – ?

Were there a God
and in the flesh,
and could he call me, I would
walk around, I would
wait a little.

Mickiewicz

I stand before the oak-wood, the castle
silent, my mother
placed a candle
beneath the ikon at the Vilna gate, sails flew
on the river, in the smoke,
the hawk swept
across the blue, a red
evening has followed him

and a time of the towns
and a time of the streets, the rock–fall
Crimea, the dust of the road
rose beside the sea,
the wagon came through the steppe
from Akkerman.

I accustom myself to luck,
I say, it is quite easy,
I think, my voice carries,
I drink a rain, I lay
my head back on the wall
Paris, I drink the sky
like a mouth, I see
the hawk that the air
lifts over the oak-wood, the river
curves in a bow down
the plains, gone,
under the swallow-airs,
gone, from the dripping dawn,
taut over the villages
and the woods: the day,
shining with wrath, an armour –

I shall come, tired from the
singsong, from the chatter, only the flight
of an étude upon my ear, I shall stand
on the slopes, listen
for a call and search for the note
with trembling mouth,
say: it is quite easy.

from *Weathersigns*

J.S.Bach

A difficult man,
town musique mentality, with sword
as well as inclination to sentiment
(where applicable of course)
a child's delight
at plashing waters, ever
effective course of rivers;
thus both bleak Jordan
and Euphrates
pregnant with heaven
are pleasant to him.

That he saw the bay –
and one there who followed
behind fires invisible,
who called the planets
with an old anguish –

sometimes
in his brilliant playing at Köthen,
in the civic pomp
of the Leipzig years
this surfaces. In the end
he could no longer hear
the spirit of Pentecost
descending with trumpet
or trombone (at 16 feet).

Flutes precede him
as weary with writing
he steps out of his
ancient house,
feels the flying
wind, knows the earth
no more.

Pike Time

Roots,
hold me,
roots of the ash-tree,
I fall from the realm of earth, veined
stone, which the wing of a swallow
brushed! Whitebreast, swallow,
fly on the path of mist.

I tore the bitter pike
loose from the bed of the stream,
struck it against a stone,
before its green grew pale,
I bound
burdock leaves round the blood.

Boat,
take me across.
The sky is white. A tree
of birdcalls
opens its eyes.

Mozart

The buckle is loose
on my shoe, there was
a silver button there,
my throat hurts me, my eyes,
if I closed them –

Then I noticed
the new wrinkle
in Colloredo's face . . .
the little house in Prague
floating down the slope,
bushes, a white wave,
in front of it – when the endless
rain was over, the light
one evening
on Stein's piano.

There was still a music
to be written,
wood, a thudding, earthly,
beneath the feet, a door
bangs in the house, I do not question,
I alone hear it,
I do not like it when Constanze
laughs
with her glassy mouth.

Midstream

Drifting down with the rafts,
in the lighter grey of the strange
shore, in a
splendour, which withdraws, in the grey
of slanting surfaces, light
shot at us from mirrors.

The Baptist's head
lay on its torn brow,
a hand with loose bluish
nails clawing
the ragged hair.

When I loved you, restless
your heart, the food on the beating
fire, your mouth, which opened,
open, the river
was a rain and flew
with the herons, leaves
fell and filled its bed.

We bent over numbed
fish, the cricket's song,
clad in scales, crossed
the sand from the foliage
of the bank, we had come
to sleep, Noman
circled the bed, Noman
extinguished the mirrors, Noman
will wake us
in our time.

Midnight Village

In the many-angled sky
Saturn plods with heavy feet
through the shadows
and whistles his moons.

It could have been seen
through the broken roof, but
the house full of sleep
like the sleep of forests
stirs in sleep,
the birds sleep on its breath
with open wings.

Let us sleep each
other's sleep and not
hear the stars and all the
voices in the darkness, the blood
only as it falls and sinks back
with red-edged, blackish
leaves under the heart.

In the morning you may strew
ashes across the sky
before the approaching
footsteps of Saturn.

The Latvian Autumn

The thicket of deadly nightshade
is open, he steps
into the clearing, the dance
of the hens round the birch-stumps is forgotten, he walks
past the tree round which the herons flew, he has sung
in the meadows.

Oh that the swath of hay,
where he lay in the bright night,
might fly scattered by winds
on the banks –

when the river is no longer awake,
the clouds above it, voices
of birds, calls:
We shall come no more.

Then I light you your light,
which I cannot see, I placed
my hands above it, close
round the flame, it stood still,
reddish in nothing but night
(like the castle which fell
in ruins over the slope,
like the little winged snake
of light through the river, like the hair
of the Jewish child)
and did not burn me.

With Wings

Do not ask, Roundeye, Whitebrow,
it was in front of your
house, I came at dusk:
the creatures soft,
made of hands and snake's hair,
voices like barking dogs
above the street.

Eyelash, do not ask, and eyebrow
let the arch suffice,
do not move your hands,
fire is a form,
no hearth
will hold it.

Wind
melts
and rain congeals,
a drawing in the water:
Love, standing with rigid
arms on the shell
abandoned by the snail

and without gesture
and hearing destroyed
in petrification – high
above the head
with wings
the darkness.

Novgorod

(ARRIVAL OF THE SAINTS)

Now,
as day breaks, the light
steps on to the banks, the lake
rises, a cloud,
black the birds
round its wings and white,

where the ikon, wooden,
floated, a green wood
and a dark face,
Nikolai, a wave
bore it with green fingers
down into the river,

and there came
Anthony, the stranger, a stone
bears him along on the waveless
water, carried a man,
he reached the bank easily,
he had seen the city,

towers and roofs,
above the mountains the walls
rising and falling in the flight
of the black and white birds,
and one tower, drawn
up against the sky.

Amen. A cross has fallen
across my path,
says Anthony, a stone . . .

Fool, go, fool, you too,
Fools, go, holy children,
across the bridge which trembles.

They walk with sticks, rags
flap on wasted arms,
windbirds, old, from the winters.

You come shouting down the road.
Lift the stone for me.

Shadow Land

The rustling voices,
leaves, I came
three ways
before a great snow.
On the bank, burrs and awns
in her ringlets, Ragana with her hounds
shouted for the ferryman, he stood
in the water, midstream.

Once,
following the mists
across the dell with golden wings,
the bustards flew, they set
horny feet on the grass,
light, the day, flew after them.

Cold. On the tip of a grass-blade
the emptiness, white,
reaching to the sky. But the tree
old, there is
a shore, mists with thin
bones move on the river.

Darkness, whoever lives here
speaks with the bird's voice.
Lanterns have glided
above the forests.
No breath has moved them.

To Klopstock

If I did not want
what is real, this: I say
river and forest,
but I have woven
into my senses the darkness,
voice of the hastening bird, the bowshot
of light round the slope

and the sounding waters –
how would I
speak your name
if a small fame
found me – I have
gathered what I passed,
the shadowed fable of guilt
and atonement:
just as the deeds
I trust – you guided it – I trust
the language of those who forget,
deep into winters
unwinged, I speak its word
of reed.

Experience

Signs,
cross and fish,
drawn on the stone wall of the cave.

The procession of men
descends into the earth.
The ground vaults,
weed, greenish, grown
through the bushes.

The river rises   .
against my breast,
the voice of sand:

open
I can not get through
your dead
drift in me

Encounter

From the overhanging tree
I called
the angry fish by name.
Round the white moon I drew
a figure, winged.
I dream the hunter's dream,
that he couple with a deer.

Clouds move over the river,
that is my voice,
snowlight over the woods,
that is my hair.
I came along
across the gloomy sky,
grass–blade in mouth, my shadow
leant on the fence, it said:
Take me back.

Tolmingkehmen Village

The noon fires burnt low,
smoke above the linden,
there he walks with white hair,
the people say:
Evening is coming soon,
someone begins the singing,
the fields bear it forth.

Come a bit further, Donelaitis,
the stream wants to rise with wings,
a hawk, enemy of the dove,
the forest, black-headed,
stands erect, the wind
calls over the hill.
There the grasses live.

This day too will descend
beneath the gibbet-shadows
of the wells, the window-light
windless, mouse-voiced
the kindling-pine
recites the blessing.

Write at the head of the page:
The sky rained grace,
and I saw Justice
waiting, that she might descend
and wrath come.

Towpath

Above the slope the wood,
stag-headed. Who walks there
lives in the berry bushes.
Around fir-shoot and fern
the earth-spider's journey. We

went along the river
to push the wood from the bank.
Float away, wood, travel
without bark. At noon
the resting-place in the shadows.
Evening comes swiftly.
Land of the crowing cocks
you flood with lights.

Someone has written
on the peeling bark of the birch:
I came in fiery traces
and trod the snow's escape route.
We too read that
and stood and waved to the birds.

Meadowbrook

The summer is cold, light
travels with sails, the fish
with fins
stands on the shadow track.

I have grown to hear
the spring in the calamus-heart,
white and reddish, the dilation,
I come, and the water-tick
pauses, the fish
plunged in its own gleam
across the depths.

Listen, I am here, I move
about
in the cold of summer.

Sanctuary

Light, falling
with the curve
of the burdock-leaf, the line of light –
Wind, the glassy wing
stirs on the bank.

Come and go and come again,
come and stay, a house,
a house of mist, stands before the forest,
roofs of smoke,
towers of birdcalls,
birch-branches secure the door at evening.

Restless we lie there,
a shawl of shadows on our shoulders,
the breezes move round
the fishermen's fires
with reddish fins,
you speak, alien voice,
I hear you with alien ear.

The Volga Towns

The stretch of wall.
Towers. The slope of the bank. Once
the wooden bridge broke. Tartar fires moved
through the plains. Night came talking,
a wandering friar with a straggly
beard. The mornings
leapt up, the cisterns
stood full of blood.

Walk about on the stone.
Here in the glassy noon
Minin raised his hand
to shade his eyes. Then shouts
flew up, towards the water, Stenka's
arrival – the Siberians walk
on the bank, up to their waists
in the undergrowth, their
forests follow them.

There
I heard
a human mouth calling:
Come into your house
through the bricked-up door,
fling open the windows
against the sea of light.

With Your Voice

The meadow-bush speaks
with your voice
late into the night, lights
fly round it.
High, a water-blossom
moves through the darkness.
The river breathes
with its creatures.

Into the calamus
I carry my plaited house.
The snail,
inaudible,
moves across my roof.
Inscribed
upon my palms
I find your face.

The End of the Summer Night

The head of the thistle
strikes at the lights
above the water. A bird
has drawn signs
into the ash-leaves. Around roots
of rush and reed
the fish spreads the red of its fins.

Dust
has risen
against fame.
Dust steps from the pillars
of mist into the plains, across
the rivers, dark
it touches the fires.

Calamus

The water-wind, a howl,
flies around
with sails of rain.
A blue dove
has spread its wings
across the wood.
Lovely in the broken iron
of the fern
the light moves
with the head of a pheasant.

Breath,
I send you out,
find a roof,
enter through a window, regard
yourself in the white mirror,
turn without sound,
a green sword.

The Towns on the Baltic Sea

The light not rising not setting.
The water that revives at the death of the moth.
Rain is rain.
The wind that comes in squalls
below the cloud
has combed the sand of the rivers, led
a dune across the sea.

Light
returns
across the water. Rain
finds the way
that the birds took. Coloured tablets
are set up
in the high crumbling walls
throughout the land.
There it can be read:
The grass grew.

The Water

You still speak
water, you speak,
you walked with small steps through
the bushes beneath the wind;
the wind sought the rivers behind
the darkness and the boat
in which the moon sails, in the hay,
you heard it saying:
Here are the willows
here the house of the owls.

But the moon looks out on the fires of Sinai.
But the water hears the frosts coming from Scythia.
But the flocks of birds rise above the forest.
But snow erects its roof against the sky.

Exodus of the Gods

Water-voice
walks on the wind,
the leap of light
is alive, a clearing,
on stones – there

cattle with dripping
mouths, garlands dragging
from horns along
bent necks – you my soul,

soul of forests,
those who hunted through you move
unarmed, the clangorous
flocks above them, there is
a singing on the reed lake, voice
black, shod,
trampling the bank,

voice which they followed
with dripping mouths
round the thorn thicket, they cropped
the bitter grass,
swaying – they sang
a lot in those days, they came
on wheels of fire
down the slopes, the banks
shone, with open eye
leaves struck in the air – this last
pronounces our end.

Language

The tree
greater than the night
with the breath of the valley lakes
with the whisper above
the stillness

The stones
beneath the feet
the shining veins
long in the dust
for ever

Language
worn out
by the weary mouth
on the endless road
to the neighbour's house

In the Empty Mirror

In the waters of light,
the brows, against each other,
the summer undergrowth
springs up above your hips, I
call down lightnings, you come
from afar lightnings, ashes,
flakes of ash
fall from you, your gown.

I was at your shoulder,
the vein on your neck
broke in my mouth, you
will not sink, I hold you
by the arms, I lift
you across the deep,
walk ahead of me.

One day: I shall bring you
the drink again, I shall fly
against the skies, one day: but I shall
descend, you will hear me
breathing, the fields will hear you
above the wind, a white light
will speak to you.

When the Rooms

When the rooms are deserted
in which answers are given, when
the walls and narrow passes fall, shadows
fly out of the trees, when the grass
beneath the feet is abandoned,
white soles tread the wind –

the bush of thorn flames,
I hear its voice,
where no question was, the waters
move, but I do not thirst.

Place of Fire

We saw that sky. Blackness
moved on the river, the fires
beat, darkness with trembling
lights stepped forward in front
of the wood on the bank, in animal hide.
We heard
the mouths in the foliage.

That sky stood
unmoved. And was made
of storms and tore us forward,
screaming we saw the earth
ascending with fields and rivers,
forest, the flying fires
benumbed.

The river remained deep. The pungence
of damp grass
rose. The voice of the cricket
lifted behind us, there was
a tree behind us,
the black alder.

We saw the sky that
perished in the darkness, sky
of fields and flying ancient
groves. Steps came
across the marsh, they
stamped out the fires.

Bird's Nest

My sky
interchanges with yours,
so does my dove
now
it flies over yours,
I see two shadows
falling
in the oatfield.

We look with
each other's eyes,
we find
a place:
rain
we say
like a story
the half-sentence
green,
I hear:

Your mouth
with the speech
of birds
carries twigs and feathers
up to my brow.

Jakub Bart in Ralbitz

Owlcries –
thus the villages
talk in the night, how shall I speak
that you may hear me,
Sorbs, the strangers are coming,
they say:
you are dead, you are
few, learn to be silent,
lie down in your graves.

But keep watch
that you may hear
your brothers beyond the border,
above the hills like fire,
above the forests, the storms
range
fraternally, you hear:
they talk with your mouths,
they walk the earth like you,
like you they come up
from the pits.

But who
have I become
that I speak?
"Woe star, you have
fallen into darkness,
into the uproar
from the blue height, the height
without sound" –
I lift myself
to that height,
I am lifted by my people
which found its voice.

Arrival

I

My door
called you, I closed
the window, covered the broken
pane, the cloud
– a roof under sinking breezes –
rose, the mallows bloomed
through the straw, I took the light
from the rain, the light
from the beating water, thus I burnt
the darkness in the house.

Beneath the door,
the cheek
questioned the mouth, the shoulder
answered the thigh:
Then you flew away, Autumn
was still visible. Winter
moved with the lights, red
fires, you lived on strangeness.
Green, a crack appeared in the ice.
There was a groaning on the river.
White on the snow.

II

He who approached you, I,
does not say: See me coming.

> White on the road
> you walked, the white calls
> of the villages flew, the green
> voice of the bank,

raspberry canes
grew up through our
hands. White and green.

Who then stands
behind the doors, listens:
A tapping
moves under the roof?

He who stands
before the gate, the living man,
will speak here, he will say:

Whoever walks this road,
enter!

Answer

Above the fence
your talk:
From the trees the burden falls,
the snow.

And in the fallen elder
the trilling of blackbirds, the crickets'
grassy voice
notches chinks into the wall. Swallow-flight
steep against the rain, constellations
move in the sky,
in the hoarfrost.

They that bury me
beneath the roots
will hear:
he speaks
to the sand
that fills his mouth – so the sand
will speak, and
the stone will cry
and the water fly.

Nightfisher

In lovely leaves
the silence
still rankling.
Light
with hands
above a wall.
The sand spills from the roots.
Sand, go away
red in the water,
go on the track of voices,
go in the dark,
spread the catch at dawn.
The voices sing silverpale,
take your ears
into safety,
into the lively leaves,
the voices sing:
dead is dead.

Beachcomber

Noon still
flaming
over the land of reeds, not
yet the rush of swans
above the dunes, still
the saltwort
silent,
the hands in the sand.

When the constellation flies
over the straits,
ice at its wings,
the forests of cricket-voices
mount
above the waste,
speaking with hollow mouths
down to the sea –

I hear you coming, you step
from your shadows, throwing
the load of driftwood
from your shoulder, a fire
flits from your hand.

I shall ask you:
What is my name?
Who am I?
How long
shall I stay here?

Names for the Persecuted

He who enters
repeats in the curtained window
the names that I give him,
names of birds and the name of the preying eel.

gerwe he says
like a crane's feather stroking the air,
angurys like a shadow approaching
under the water.

In the end I give him
the name "Eldertree", the name
of the inaudible, which
is ripe
and stands full of blood.

To Jawlensky

When the water falls,
under the birdcries
the land becomes visible.
The red too sinks
under the wings.

I have seen a line
in my own eye,
the track of a snail, the breath
above the snow,
earth's brow grown
white, a moss.

By Day

He who sings with his hands
has turned away
the airs open
and answer
with mouths of gold

There is a lovely silence
we shall go down
and tell the fishermen
set sail now
do not wait for the night

Esther

This is
my people.
Which disperses
among the peoples
and sits at the gate.

The wild-faced one
stands erect
on the stones, he lets
the lands rest, the gold
moves with flames
above his head, he hears me:

If I perish
I perish, I was afraid,
your glory runs
with lightnings through the sky,
the leaping blood
of trumpets
builds my house.

Crypt / Brandenburg Cathedral

Here
the vessel for the darkness:
clattering, but the walls
broken open against
the shadows and white lights,
there the trees
pass
with bare heads.

Old, darkness, do
not go under the earth,
do not go down,
hold your breath, your cry:
Who will cover my eyes, who
will lift my arms, who
will carry my hair?

That the evening, you say,
may not come – it comes with the smoke
on the water, it calls
its name without sound
from the other shore –

that it may not come, strike
the stone on the rim of the bell: thus
the heroine will ring out
brazenly, at her call
wingless
the air will
stand and will walk around
unshod.

Town

They perceive, who demanded
your blood, they perceive:
the wound still festers.
Mist covers
the sharp edges. The polonaise
of the bald-headed
lamps begins. And the snow
comes too.

Here
the stones leap, painted
walls, the staircase
breaks, around the dead pigeons
– their standards –
the armies of rats form up.

Here
they say,
a tree will green
and hold the sky,
they say,
on leaves and branches.

Kolno Dance

He dances in the room,
small steps on the sanded boards,
as he lifts his foot his laughter
trembles – a linen cloth –
in front of him,
in front of his tears.

The horses in the window
move their heads, the trilling
of a goldfinch rises to the beams,
red and blue the hollyhocks
speak across the fence:
A rain that will weep for us
is coming soon.

Why weep, asks the laughter.
Why laugh, ask the tears.

You make my feet dance,
one to the right,
one to the left,
both to the right,
both to the left,
both ahead on the road:
where the light moves by the river,
goes away over the fields,
flies up over the forest –

But speak.
Now he will speak no more.

The Bird, White

The bird, white,
which a breath of the air
bore out beyond its death,
the bird with pale feathers
hangs lustreless
above the hill, above
a birch, above its own
shadow. The shadow rose
from the water
on to the sand.

And now
a church with coffins
beneath its roof,
with red and white stones
at its feet. Voices,
mouths of smoke,
speak in the foliage

of feathers,
of white wings,
of a bird "eyeless".

House

I

Across the roof moves the light,
wants to follow the blackbirds' flight.
At the wall the elders stand
blotting out the lines of a hand.
The larkspur in its bed
does not hear what I said.
"Here I will lay me down", the rain
writes on the ridge-pole this refrain.

II

At the wall the shadows
talk with voices:
How shall we dress
for the day?

A flower that trembles
in the hair, a green
tendril above the eyes,
a clover-leaf at the breast.

Step forward shadows,
the light wants to begin with small
steps, show it
the way.

Down the slope,
as the cocks cry fire
across the roofs,
while the animals talk
their old talk,
but with leaps,
across the sandy yard.

Shadows, go from the door now.
Shadows, now go from the windows.
Go from beneath the roof.
Shadow of trembling tendril,
vineleaf shadow, I want
to hear shadows, speak:
You are going to stay here
for a time.

Reawakening

The land
empty,
through spread sheets
the other land, laid
below, only
suspected before,
rises green. It comes
from the time of plague, white
with bones, ribs, vertebrae,
radii, calcified.

Count
the grasses
and count
threads of rainwater
and light, count
the little leaves, and leave
your footprints, deertracks,
and voices, revive
with words
the blood in the trees and
lungs, knock
the rust from walls
and steps,
it will cling
to your hands, may feed
there
on your nails.

It is not the time to ask.
It is the time for the water
on the shoots, for the renewed
conjunction of leaves, and may foliage
open eyes.

Silcher's Grave

At one side, the bench in front of the wall,
in the leafy shadow, cross and small tree
above the grave: in the long silence
which began after the songs of friendship

and outsang time and name. There is a residue
of dead voices, hands, as though fallen
unopened into the lap. No question
more to be heard, none answered.

With the Songs of Sappho

Pursed the hairy
lips, from the island
the skinny girl cries out
like a mule:

    a peplos,
    saffron-coloured, wreaths
    Phrygian, purple

Solon
before the house
where the air circles:
Sing it again, he says,

that I may learn the
island cries, the calls
close to the earth
in the burnt weed,

learn it, and die
while learning, words
have and words, the rushing,
the zephyr behind the head and,
words, above the breast.

The Deserted House

The avenue
defined
by the footsteps of the dead. How the echo
descended over the sea
of air, beneath the trees
ivy creeps, the roots
show, the silence
approaches with birds, white voices.
In the house
walked shadows, a strange conversation
beneath the window. The mice
scurry
through the broken spinet.
I saw an old woman
at the end of the road
in a black shawl
on the stone,
she looked southwards.
Above the sand
with hard split leaves
the thistle bloomed.
There the sky was
opened, in the colour of children's hair.
Earth of beauty fatherland.

Precaution

Attacks of dipsomania.
They come like silence
comes.

The map
pinned on the wall,
a name underlined,
the undiscovered city,
the roads to it
charted.

Burdock,
grow great leaves,
sure safeguard.

Undine

From her shadows
rises
the unspoken speech,
from the leaves
a curving arm.

You step on to a bridge.
You carry a flower in your mouth.
You hide near the towers.
You cast the leaping pebble forth.

I have no fire.
The birds sleep in the straw.
Wings and feeding-cries
live audibly in the roof.

   Breath,
carry me.
   Darkness,
speak with your hands.
The sound of water builds nests
into the feathered silence.
Under the water the houses
stand with open doors,
windows, a staircase
of stone looms up.

Blood Rain

Above us,
before they began to fly,
lifted by the wind,
opening
against the sky,
the blossoms
are drowned,

fallen
with flying water,
dust-coloured.
Your hair is like grass.

Take my breath which
divides blood
and water,

new eyelids
for a day.

Mobile by Calder

White metal
held in the air
by mists
white
a motion
we lend it wings

Your mouth
has opened as a rose
leaves rustle
at your temples

Estrangement

Time
walks around
clad
in good luck
and bad luck

Time clad in bad luck
speaks with the clatter
of storks, the storks
avoid him: his plumage
black, his trees shadows,
there is night, his roads
run through the air.

To Hölty

May dance
or The Shepherdess –
cry of leaves round the laurel,
whorl, in the frost
smoke.
The breath
gone through water.

There was a ford,
sandy, eddies whirled, the light
numb. There was a tree.
Evening. A mouth
which denied itself salt.

Was your voice.
May song,
under the earth.

The Word "Man"

The word "man", to be found
as a word; where it belongs,
in the OED:
between mamzer and manaass.

The city
old and new,
lovely and lively, with trees
too
and vehicles, here

I hear the word, I hear
the word often here, I can
name those who use it, I can
begin to.

Where there is no love
do not utter the word.

Notes

The notes are the author's, except those marked with an asterisk, which are the translators'.

Sarmatian Time

THE JURA (p. 27)
Jura: an eastern tributary of the River Memel.
Nemona: the Latvian name for the River Memel.

*THE WIVES OF THE NEHRUNG-FISHERS (p. 29)
Nehrung: spit of land separating a Haff from the sea.

TO THE JEWISH DEALER A.S. (p. 31)
Rasainen: a small Lithuanian country town.

WAGON TRIP (p. 34)
Mariampol: town in Lithuania.

THE LOG-CABIN ABOVE THE VILIA (p. 35)
Vilia: eastern tributary of the River Memel.

VILNA (p. 36)
Giedimin: Grand Duke, a figure in early Lithuanian history.
Njemen: the Russian name for the River Memel.
Lizdejko: legendary singer.
Trakai: a castle belonging to the rulers of Lithuania on an island in Lake Trakai, now a ruin.

BY THE RIVER (p. 38)
Ostra Brama: a gate in Vilna, an ancient place of pilgrimage with a miracle-working picture of the Virgin Mary.

DEAD LANGUAGE (p. 41)
The poem uses words from the language of the Pruzzians which became extinct in the eighteenth century and of which only fragments survive.

PRUZZIAN ELEGY (p. 47)
The poem invokes the memory of the Pruzzians who were exterminated by the Teutonic Knights.
Perkun, Pikoll, Patrimpe: Pruzzian gods.

*Mourning for Jahnn (p. 49)
Hans Henny Jahnn (1894–1959). German pacifist writer and musician.

*Günderode (p. 52)
Karoline von Günderode (1780–1806). German poetess of the romantic period.

*The Singing Swan (p. 55)
Singschwan – Cygnus cygnus – Whooper swan.

Village Road (p. 57)
Ryazan: former administrative district called after the town of the same name near Moscow.
Mikula: the holy ploughman, legendary figure.
Chadayev: author and philosopher, a contemporary of Pushkin.

On the Tauric Road (p. 59)
Enkidu: a figure in the epic of Gilgamesh.

Landscape with Birds (p. 60)
Temujin: Genghis Khan.

Latvian Songs (p. 66)
A Herr von Uexküll appeared before the city council in Riga in the seventeenth century, charged with murdering one of his servants.

The Memel (p. 76)
Jura, Mitva, Szeszupe: tributaries of the Memel.

The Daubas (p. 78)
Lithuanian name for the left bank of the Memel near Ragnit.

Recall (p. 82)
Perkun: see "Pruzzian Elegy".

Shadowland Rivers

The Call of the Quail (p. 85)
For the interpretation of the quail's call by the anapaest "Lobet Gott" (God be praised) see F.L. Mittler, *Deutsche Volkslieder* (Frankfurt am Main, 1865), no. 606, p. 467.
*kurgan: a prehistoric sepulchral tumulus or barrow in Russia and Tartary.

TALE (p. 94)
Kiteshgorod: according to the legend a drowned city in Lake Svetlojar near Rybinsk (Upper Volga).

HAMANN (p. 99)
Johann Georg Hamann in Königsberg (1730–1788).
Wasianski: then priest to the local Polish congregation.
The author of *Lives According to a Rising Line* was Th. G. Hippel; the author of *Poems in the Style of Grécourt* was J.G. Scheffner; both books were published anonymously.
Lizentgraben: where Hamann lived, *Katzbach:* where he was born.

LAMENT (p. 105)
The poem is addressed to Dietrich Buxtehude.

*BRENTANO IN ASCHAFFENBURG (p. 108)
Clemens Brentano (1778–1842). He arrived in Aschaffenburg shortly before his death.

*HÖLDERLIN IN TÜBINGEN (p. 109)
Friedrich Hölderlin (1770–1843). Died in Tübingen.

*BIRD ROUTES 1957 (p. 113)
Väinemöinen (Väinämöinen): hero of the Finnish national epos "Kalevala".

GERTRUD KOLMAR (p. 114)
girded about with towers is a quotation from Gertrud Kolmar's poem "The Jewess".
*Gertrud Kolmar, born 1894. German poetess of Jewish descent. Deported 1943. The date and place of her death are unknown.

*ELSE LASKER-SCHÜLER (p. 115)
Else Lasker-Schüler (1869–1945). German poetess of Jewish descent. She was buried on the Mount of Olives.

*TO NELLY SACHS (p. 116)
Nelly Sachs (1891–1970). German poetess of Jewish descent. Nobel Prize for Literature 1966.
Perun: heathen god.

*THE DON (p. 118)
Div: a spirit, a bearer of evil tidings who appears in the form of a bird.

*MICKIEWICZ (p. 138)
Adam Mickiewicz (1798–1855). Polish national poet.

Weathersigns

J.S. BACH (p. 143)
The second verse refers to Bach's visit to Buxtehude in Lübeck.

*SHADOW LAND (p. 152)
Ragana: originally a seer in Lithuanian-Latvian mythology, later a sorceress who inflicts harm on humans and animals.

*TO KLOPSTOCK (p. 153)
Friedrich Gottlieb Klopstock (1724–1803). German poet.

TOLMINGKEHMEN VILLAGE (p. 156)
Christian Donelaitis (Donalitius) was parson in Tolmingkehmen from 1743 until his death in 1780. His idylls ("The Seasons"), which portray the life of the Lithuanian people, stand at the beginning of Lithuanian literature.

*THE VOLGA TOWNS (p. 160)
Minin: Kusma Minin, leading citizen of Novgorod in the early seventeenth century.
Stenka: Stenka Razin, leader of Cossack revolt in 1671.

JAKUB BART IN RALBITZ (p. 172)
Jakub Bart-Ćišinski (1856–1919), the Sorbian national poet. He came as a young priest in Spring 1883 to Ralbitz, "the poorest parish in the world". The quotation is a free translation of two lines of his poem "O tempora O mores".

NAMES FOR THE PERSECUTED (p. 178)
The two Pruzzian words mean: *gerwe* = crane, *angurys* = eel, the so-called "broad-headed".

*TO JAWLENSKY (p. 179)
Alexei Jawlensky (1864-1941). German-Russian painter.

*SILCHER'S GRAVE (p. 189)
Friedrich Silcher (1789–1860). German composer of choral music.

*TO HÖLTY (p. 196)
Ludwig Christoph Heinrich Hölty (1748–1776). German poet.

Johannes Bobrowski: a note

JOHANNES BOBROWSKI was born on 9 April 1917 in Tilsit in East Prussia, and grew up, as he himself said, "on both sides of the River Memel". At that time the northern shore of the river was Lithuanian, the southern shore German. The son of a German railwayman, Bobrowski spent part of his boyhood on his grandfather's farm in Lithuania, in an area where Germans, Lithuanians, Poles, Russians and Jews – the latter forming a large proportion of the population – lived side by side. He was educated in Rastenburg and Königsberg and was studying art history at the Humboldt University in Berlin when he was conscripted in 1939. He took part in the military campaigns in Poland, France and Russia. He married in 1943 Johanna Buddrus.

Bobrowski began to write poetry on the Eastern Front in 1941 where as a 24-year-old German soldier in Kaunas he saw the "slavering wolves" of the SS drive the "grey processions" over a hill to death, a process for which he found a historical parallel, "the clash between the Teutonic Knights and the peoples of the East, Prussian policy in Eastern Europe". Bobrowski published his first poems, which he never reprinted, in *Das Innere Reich*, the Nazi cultural periodical, in 1943. His poems next appeared in the East Berlin Communist magazine *Sinn und Form* ten years later.

Bobrowski was a prisoner-of-war in Russia, where he worked as a coalminer, until 1949 when he returned to a Berlin as yet undivided by a wall. The hard and heavy years had worked him over. He rejoined his family in Friedrichshagen and became an editor at the publishing house of Lucie Groszer and in 1959 at Union Verlag in East Berlin. He began to write with a purpose which was avowedly didactic: "to tell my countrymen what they still do not know about their eastern neighbours".

Most of Bobrowski's poems are set in a part historical, part mythical, part contemporary, part imagined land – Sarmatia. The name is still to be found in the encyclopedias. It was a land known to Roman historians, a country of nomads stretching from the Vistula and the Danube to the Volga and the Caucasus, an empire founded in 400 BC and overthrown eight centuries later by the Goths. But it was also the land of Bobrowski's childhood and his captivity. The didactic purpose of Bobrowski's poetry is surpassed by the supreme fiction of his Sarmatia, a land of lost content, creating what never was and preserving what cannot be.

Bobrowski published his first book of poetry, *Sarmatian Time*, in 1961 and his work quickly acquired a wide reputation. In 1962 he was awarded the West German Gruppe 47 prize and the Austrian Alma Johanna Koenig prize, in 1965 the East German Heinrich Mann prize and the Swiss Charles Veillon prize. His work has been much translated especially into the languages of his "eastern neighbours". He wrote four volumes of poetry – *Sarmatische Zeit* (1961), *Schattenland Ströme* (1962), *Wetterzeichen* (1966) and *Im Windgesträuch* (1970); two novels – *Levins Mühle* (1964) and *Litauische Claviere* (1966); and several collections of stories – *Mäusefest* (1965), *Boehlendorff* (1965) and *Der Mahner* (1967). A collection of satirical verses *Literarisches Klima* appeared in 1977.

Johannes Bobrowski died in East Berlin on 2 September 1965; an early death, but not untypical in his broken generation.

M.M.   1984

Index of Titles

Above the River, 124
Always to be Named, 137
The Animals at Christmas, 96
Answer, 175
Arrival, 173
At the River, 91

Beachcomber, 177
Bird Routes 1957, 113
Bird's Nest, 171
The Bird, White, 185
Blood Rain, 194
Brentano in Aschaffenburg, 108
By Day, 180
By the River, 38

Calamus, 163
Call, 23
The Call of the Quail, 85
Cails, 89
Cathedral 1941, 125
Childhood, 25
The Church: Comfort My
    Affliction, 58
Cloister Near Novgorod, 128
Counterlight, 46
Crypt/Brandenburg Cathedral, 182

The Daubas, 78
Dead Language, 41
The Death of the Wolf, 98
The Deserted House, 191
Deserted Township, 120
The Don, 118
Dryad, 90
The Duna, 67
Dylan Thomas, 54

The Eagle, 87
Easter, 130
Elder-Blossom, 100
Else Lasker-Schüler, 115
Encounter, 155
The End of the Summer Night, 162
Esther, 181
Estrangement, 195
Exodus of the Gods, 166
Experience, 154

Fire and Snow, 73
Fishingport, 30
The Ford, 133
French Village, 107
From the Rivers, 111

Gertrud Kolmar, 114
Góngora, 51
Graveyard, 40
Günderode, 52

Hamann, 99
The Hawk, 71
Hölderlin in Tübingen, 109
The Homeland of the Painter
    Chagall, 65
House, 186

Ikons, 119
In the Empty Mirror, 168
In Memory of B.L., 132
In Transit, 123

Jakub Bart in Ralbitz, 172
Joseph Conrad, 53
J.S. Bach, 143
The Jura, 27

Kaunas 1941, 69
Kolno Dance, 184

Lake Ilmen 1941, 62
Lake Shore, 74
Lament, 105
Landscape with Birds, 60
Language, 167
The Latvian Autumn, 148
Latvian Songs, 66
Lithuanian Songs, 43
The Lithuanian Well, 39
Log-Cabin, 134
The Log-Cabin Above the Vilia, 35

Meadowbrook, 158
The Memel, 76
Memorial Leaf, 102
Mickiewicz, 138
Midnight Village, 147

Midstream, 146
Mobile by Calder, 195
Mourning for Jahnn, 49
Mozart, 145

Names for the Persecuted, 178
Nightfisher, 176
Night-Swallows, 110
Nightway, 68
North Russian Town, 122
Novgorod (Arrival of the Saints),
   150
Nymph, 26

One Day, 75
On the Tauric Road, 59

Pike Time, 144
Place of Fire, 170
Plain, 88
Precaution, 192
Pruzzian Elegy, 47

Reawakening, 188
Recall, 82
Report, 127
Return, 72
River Poem, 63
The Road Home, 136
The Road of the Armies, 32
Russian Songs, 131

Sanctuary, 159
The Sarmatian Plain, 44
Sea-Piece, 106
Silcher's Grave, 189
The Singing Swan, 55
Shadow Land, 152
The Spoor in the Sand, 42
Steppe, 61

Summer Cries, 92

Tale, 94
To Hölty, 196
To Jawlensky, 179
To Klopstock, 153
Tolmingkehmen Village, 156
The Tomsk Road, 129
To Nelly Sachs, 116
To the Chassid Barkan, 101
To the Jewish Dealer A.S., 31
Town, 183
The Towns on the Baltic Sea, 164
Towpath, 157

Under the Edge of Night, 121
Undine, 193
Unsaid, 93

Village, 24
Village Church 1942, 126
Village Music, 135
Village Road, 57
Villon, 50
Vilna, 36
The Volga Towns, 160

Wagon Trip, 34
The Wanderer, 95
The Water, 165
Weathersigns, 103
When the Rooms, 169
Windmill, 56
Winter Cries, 97
Winterlight, 80
With the Songs of Sappho, 190
With Wings, 149
With Your Voice, 161
The Wives of the Nehrung-Fishers, 29
The Word "Man", 197

New Directions Paperbooks—A Partial Listing

Walter Abish, *How German Is It.* NDP508.
John Allman, *Scenarios for a Mixed Landscape.* NDP619.
Sherwood Anderson, *Poor White.* NDP763.
Wayne Andrews, *The Surrealist Parade.* NDP689.
David Antin, *Tuning.* NDP570.
G. Apollinaire, *Selected Writings.*† NDP310.
Jimmy S. Baca, *Martín & Meditations.* NDP648.
  Black Mesa Poems. NDP676.
Djuna Barnes, *Nightwood.* NDP98.
J. Barzun, *An Essay on French Verse.* NDP708.
H.E. Bates, *Elephant's Nest in a Rhubarb Tree.* NDP669.
  A Party for the Girls, NDP653.
Charles Baudelaire, *Flowers of Evil.*† NDP684.
  Paris Spleen. NDP294.
Bei Dao, *Old Snow.* NDP727.
  Waves. NDP693.
Gottfried Benn, *Primal Vision.* NDP322.
Adolfo Bioy Casares, *A Russian Doll.* NDP745.
Carmel Bird, *The Bluebird Café.* NDP707.
R. P. Blackmur, *Studies in Henry James,* NDP552.
Wolfgang Borchert, *The Man Outside.* NDP319.
Jorge Luis Borges, *Labyrinths.* NDP186.
  Seven Nights. NDP576.
Kay Boyle, *Life Being the Best.* NDP654.
  Fifty Stories. NDP741.
M. Bulgakov, *Flight & Bliss.* NDP593.
  The Life of M. de Moliere. NDP601.
Frederick Busch, *Absent Friends.* NDP721.
Veza Canetti, *Yellow Street.* NDP709.
Ernesto Cardenal, *Zero Hour.* NDP502.
Joyce Cary, *A House of Children.* NDP631.
  Mister Johnson. NDP631.
Hayden Carruth, *Tell Me Again. . . .* NDP677.
Louis-Ferdinand Céline,
  Death on the Installment Plan. NDP330.
  Journey to the End of the Night. NDP542.
René Char. *Selected Poems.*† NDP734.
Jean Cocteau, *The Holy Terrors.* NDP212.
M. Collis, *She Was a Queen.* NDP716.
Cid Corman, *Sun Rock Man.* NDP318.
Gregory Corso, *Long Live Man.* NDP127.
  Herald of the Autochthonic Spirit. NDP522.
Robert Creeley, *Memory Gardens.* NDP613.
  Windows. NDP687.
Edward Dahlberg, *Because I Was Flesh.* NDP227.
Alain Daniélou, *The Way to the Labyrinth.* NDP634.
Osamu Dazai, *The Setting Sun.* NDP258.
  No Longer Human. NDP357.
Mme. de Lafayette, *The Princess of Cleves.* NDP660.
E. Dujardin, *We'll in the Woods No More.* NDP682.
Robert Duncan, *Selected Poems.* NDP754.
Richard Eberhart, *The Long Reach.* NDP565.
Wm. Empson, *7 Types of Ambiguity.* NDP204.
  Some Versions of Pastoral. NDP92.
S. Endo, *The Sea and the Poison.* NDP737.
Wm. Everson, *The Residual Years.* NDP263.
Gavin Ewart, *Selected Poems.* NDP655.
Lawrence Ferlinghetti, *A Coney Island of the Mind.* NDP74.
  Starting from San Francisco. NDP220.
  Wild Dreams of a New Beginning. NDP663.
Ronald Firbank, *Five Novels.* NDP581.
  Three More Novels. NDP614.
F. Scott Fitzgerald, *The Crack-up.* NDP54.
Gustave Flaubert, *Dictionary.* NDP230.
J. Gahagan, *Did Gustav Mahler Ski?* NDP711.
Gandhi, *Gandhi on Non-Violence.* NDP197.
Gary, Romain, *Promise at Dawn.* NDP635.
  The Life Before Us ("Madame Rosa"). NDP604.
W. Gerhardie, *Futility.* NDP722.
Goethe, *Faust,* Part I. NDP70.
Allen Grossman, *The Ether Dome.* NDP723.
Martin Grzimek, *Shadowlife.* NDP705.
Guigonnat, Henri, *Daemon in Lithuania.* NDP592.
Lars Gustafsson, *The Death of a Beekeeper.* NDP523.
  A Tiler's Afternoon. NDP761.

John Hawkes, *The Beetle Leg.* NDP239.
  Humors of Blood & Skin. NDP577.
  Second Skin. NDP146.
Samuel Hazo, *To Paris.* NDP512.
H. D. *Collected Poems.* NDP611.
  Helen in Egypt. NDP380.
  HERmione. NDP526.
  Selected Poems. NDP658.
  Tribute to Freud. NDP572.
Robert E. Helbling, *Heinrich von Kleist.* NDP390.
William Herrick, *Bradovich.* NDP762.
Herman Hesse, *Siddhartha.* NDP65.
Paul Hoover, *The Novel.* NDP706.
Susan Howe, *The Nonconformist's Memorial.* NDP755.
Vicente Huidobro, *Selected Poetry.* NDP520.
C. Isherwood, *All the Conspirators.* NDP480.
  The Berlin Stories. NDP134.
Ledo Ivo, *Snake's Nest.* NDP521.
Fleur Jaeggy, *Sweet Days of Discipline.* NDP758.
Gustav Janouch, *Conversations with Kafka.* NDP313.
Alfred Jarry, *Ubu Roi.* NDP105.
Robinson Jeffers, *Cawdor and Medea.* NDP293.
B.S. Johnson, *Christie Malry's. . . .* NDP600.
  Albert Angelo. NDP628.
James Joyce, *Stephen Hero.* NDP133.
Franz Kafka, *Amerika.* NDP117.
Mary Karr, *The Devil's Tour.* NDP768.
Bob Kaufman, *The Ancient Rain.* NDP514.
H. von Kleist, *Prince Friedrich.* NDP462.
Rüdiger Kremer, *The Color of Snow.* NDP743.
Jules Laforgue, *Moral Tales.* NDP594.
P. Lal, *Great Sanskrit Plays.* NDP142.
Tommaso Landolfi, *Gogol's Wife.* NDP155.
"Language" Poetries: An Anthology. NDP630.
D. Larsen, *Stitching Porcelain.* NDP710.
James Laughlin, *The Man in the Wall.* NDP759.
Lautréamont, *Maldoror.* NDP207.
H. Leibowitz, *Fabricating Lives.* NDP715.
Siegfried Lenz, *The German Lesson.* NDP618.
Denise Levertov, *Breathing the Water.* NDP640.
  A Door in the Hive. NDP685.
  Evening Train. NDP750.
  New & Selected Essays. NDP749.
  Poems 1960-1967. NDP549.
  Poems 1968-1972. NDP629.
  Oblique Prayers. NDP578.
Harry Levin, *James Joyce.* NDP87.
Li Ch'ing-chao, *Complete Poems.* NDP492.
Enrique Lihn, *The Dark Room.*† NDP542.
C. Lispector, *Soulstorm.* NDP671.
  The Hour of the Star. NDP733.
Garciá Lorca, *Five Plays.* NDP232.
  The Public & Play Without a Title. NDP561.
  Selected Poems.† NDP114.
  Three Tragedies. NDP52.
Francisco G. Lorca, *In The Green Morning.* NDP610.
Michael McClure, *Rebel Lions.* NDP712.
  Selected Poems. NDP599.
Carson McCullers, *The Member of the Wedding.* (Playscript) NDP153.
Stéphane Mallarme,† *Selected Poetry and Prose.* NDP529.
Bernadette Mayer, *A Bernadette Mayer Reader.* NDP739.
Thomas Merton, *Asian Journal.* NDP394.
  New Seeds of Contemplation. ND337.
  Selected Poems. NDP85.
  Thomas Merton in Alaska. NDP652.
  The Way of Chuang Tzu. NDP276.
  Zen and the Birds of Appetite. NDP261.
Henri Michaux, *A Barbarian in Asia.* NDP622.
  Selected Writings. NDP264.
Henry Miller, *The Air-Conditioned Nightmare.* NDP302.
  Aller Retour New York. NDP753.
  Big Sur & The Oranges. NDP161.
  The Colossus of Maroussi. NDP75.
  A Devil in Paradise. NDP765.
  Into the Heart of Life. NDP728.
  The Smile at the Foot of the Ladder. NDP386.

For complete listing request free catalog from
New Directions, 80 Eighth Avenue, New York 10011

†Bilingual

Y. Mishima, *Confessions of a Mask.* NDP253.
 Death in Midsummer. NDP215.
Frédéric Mistral, *The Memoirs.* NDP632.
Eugenio Montale, *It Depends.*† NDP507.
 Selected Poems.† NDP193.
Paul Morand, *Fancy Goods / Open All Night.*
 NDP567.
Vladimir Nabokov, *Nikolai Gogol.* NDP78.
 Laughter in the Dark. NDP729.
 The Real Life of Sebastian Knight. NDP432.
P. Neruda, *The Captain's Verses.*† NDP345.
 Residence on Earth.† NDP340.
New Directions in Prose & Poetry (Anthology).
 Available from #17 forward to #55.
Robert Nichols, *Arrival.* NDP437.
 Exile. NDP485.
J. F. Nims, *The Six-Cornered Snowflake.* NDP700.
Charles Olson, *Selected Writings.* NDP231.
Toby Olson, *The Life of Jesus.* NDP417.
 Seaview. NDP532.
George Oppen, *Collected Poems.* NDP418.
István Örkeny, *The Flower Show /*
 The Toth Family. NDP536.
Wilfred Owen, *Collected Poems.* NDP210.
José Emilio Pacheco, *Battles in the Desert.* NDP637.
 Selected Poems.† NDP638.
Nicanor Parra, *Antipoems: New & Selected.* NDP603.
Boris Pasternak, *Safe Conduct.* NDP77.
Kenneth Patchen, *Because It Is.* NDP83.
 Collected Poems. NDP284.
 Selected Poems. NDP160.
 Wonderings. NDP320.
Ota Pavel, *How I Came to Know Fish.* NDP713.
Octavio Paz, *Collected Poems.* NDP719.
 Configurations.† NDP303.
 A Draft of Shadows.† NDP489.
 Selected Poems. NDP574.
 Sunstone.† NDP735.
 A Tree Within.† NDP661.
St. John Perse, *Selected Poems.*† NDP545.
J. A. Porter, *Eelgrass.* NDP438.
Ezra Pound, *ABC of Reading.* NDP89.
 Confucius. NDP285.
 Confucius to Cummings. (Anth.) NDP126.
 A Draft of XXX Cantos. NDP690.
 Elektra. NDP683.
 Guide to Kulchur. NDP257.
 Literary Essays. NDP250.
 Personae. NDP697.
 Selected Cantos. NDP304.
 Selected Poems. NDP66.
 The Spirit of Romance. NDP266.
Raymond Queneau, *The Blue Flowers.* NDP595.
 Exercises in Style. NDP513.
Mary de Rachewiltz, *Ezra Pound.* NDP405.
Raja Rao, *Kanthapura.* NDP224.
Herbert Read, *The Green Child.* NDP208.
P. Reverdy, *Selected Poems.*† NDP346.
Kenneth Rexroth, *An Autobiographical Novel.* NDP725.
 Classics Revisited. NDP621.
 More Classics Revisited. NDP668.
 Flower Wreath Hill. NDP724.
 100 Poems from the Chinese. NDP192.
 100 Poems from the Japanese.† NDP147.
 Selected Poems. NDP581.
 Women Poets of China. NDP528.
 Women Poets of Japan. NDP527.
Rainer Maria Rilke, *Poems from*
 The Book of Hours. NDP408.
 Possibility of Being. (Poems). NDP436.
 Where Silence Reigns. (Prose). NDP464.
Arthur Rimbaud, *Illuminations.*† NDP56.
 Season in Hell & Drunken Boat.† NDP97.
Edouard Roditi, *Delights of Turkey.* NDP445.
Jerome Rothenberg, *Khurbn.* NDP679.
 New Selected Poems. NDP625.
Nayantara Sahgal, *Rich Like Us.* NDP665.

Ihara Saikaku, *The Life of an Amorous*
 Woman. NDP270.
St. John of the Cross, *Poems.*† NDP341.
W. Saroyan, *Man With the Heart in the Highlands.*
 NDP740.
Jean-Paul Sartre, *Nausea.* NDP82.
 The Wall (Intimacy). NDP272.
P. D. Scott, *Coming to Jakarta.* NDP672.
 Listening to the Candle. NDP747.
Delmore Schwartz, *Selected Poems.* NDP241.
 In Dreams Begin Responsibilities. NDP454.
Shattan, *Manimekhalaï.* NDP674.
K. Shiraishi. *Seasons of Sacred Lust.* NDP453.
Stevie Smith, *Collected Poems.* NDP562.
 New Selected Poems. NDP659.
Gary Snyder, *The Back Country.* NDP249.
 The Real Work. NDP499.
 Regarding Wave. NDP306.
 Turtle Island. NDP381.
Muriel Spark, *The Public Image.* NDP767.
Enid Starkie, *Rimbaud.* NDP254.
Stendhal, *Three Italian Chronicles.* NDP704.
Antonio Tabucchi, *Indian Nocturne.* NDP666.
Nathaniel Tarn, *Lyrics . . . Bride of God.* NDP391.
Dylan Thomas, *Adventures in the Skin Trade.*
 NDP183.
 A Child's Christmas in Wales. NDP181.
 Collected Poems 1934-1952. NDP316.
 Collected Stories. NDP626.
 Portrait of the Artist as a Young Dog. NDP51.
 Quite Early One Morning. NDP90.
 Under Milk Wood. NDP73.
Tian Wen: *A Chinese Book of Origins.* NDP624.
Uwe Timm, *The Snake Tree.* NDP686.
Lionel Trilling, *E. M. Forster.* NDP189.
Tu Fu, *Selected Poems.* NDP675.
N. Tucci, *The Rain Came Last.* NDP688.
Paul Valéry, *Selected Writings.*† NDP184.
Elio Vittorini, *A Vittorini Omnibus.* NDP366.
Rosmarie Waldrop, *The Reproduction of Profiles.*
 NDP649.
Robert Penn Warren, *At Heaven's Gate.* NDP588.
Vernon Watkins, *Selected Poems.* NDP221.
Eliot Weinberger, *Outside Stories.* NDP751.
Nathanael West, *Miss Lonelyhearts &*
 Day of the Locust. NDP125.
J. Wheelwright, *Collected Poems.* NDP544.
Tennessee Williams, *Baby Doll.* NDP714.
 Camino Real. NDP301.
 Cat on a Hot Tin Roof. NDP398.
 Clothes for a Summer Hotel. NDP556.
 The Glass Menagerie. NDP218.
 Hard Candy. NDP225.
 A Lovely Sunday for Creve Coeur. NDP497.
 One Arm & Other Stories. NDP237.
 Red Devil Battery Sign. NDP650.
 A Streetcar Named Desire. NDP501.
 Sweet Bird of Youth. NDP409.
 Twenty-Seven Wagons Full of Cotton. NDP217.
 Vieux Carre. NDP482.
William Carlos Williams,
 The Autobiography. NDP223.
 The Buildup. NDP259.
 Collected Poems: Vol. I. NDP730
 Collected Poems: Vol. II. NDP731
 The Doctor Stories. NDP585.
 Imaginations. NDP329.
 In the American Grain. NDP53.
 In the Money. NDP240.
 Paterson. Complete. NDP152.
 Pictures from Brueghel. NDP118.
 Selected Poems (new ed.). NDP602.
 White Mule. NDP226.
Wisdom Books: *Spanish Mystics.* NDP442;
 St. Francis. NDP477; *Taoists.* NDP509;
 Wisdom of the Desert. NDP295;
 Zen Masters. NDP415.

For complete listing request free catalog from
New Directions, 80 Eighth Avenue, New York 10011

†Bilingual